Meditation in the College Classroom

Meditation in the College Classroom

A Pedagogical Tool to Help Students De-Stress, Focus, and Connect

Steve Haberlin

ROWMAN & LITTLEFIELD
Lanham • Boulder • New York • London

Published by Rowman & Littlefield
An imprint of The Rowman & Littlefield Publishing Group, Inc.
4501 Forbes Boulevard, Suite 200, Lanham, Maryland 20706
www.rowman.com

86-90 Paul Street, London EC2A 4NE, United Kingdom

British Library Cataloguing in Publication Information Available

Library of Congress Cataloging-in-Publication Data Available

ISBN 978-1-4758-7011-4 (cloth) | ISBN 978-1-4758-7012-1 (paper) | ISBN 978-1-4758-
7013-8 (ebook)

♾™ The paper used in this publication meets the minimum requirements of American
National Standard for Information Sciences—Permanence of Paper for Printed Library
Materials, ANSI/NISO Z39.48-1992.

Contents

Foreword

Miles Neale, PsyD

Higher education students are under incredible pressure these days. As this book indicates, students in the classroom are experiencing historically high rates of stress, anxiety, and depression. There is also the underlying existential angst about their uncertain future that can leave even the most resilient person despairing. Armed with new technologies, including social media, that hack and exploit our neurobiology, students are now bombarded with information and adversely influenced from every direction like puppets on a corporate, for-profit, string. They are also more distracted than ever.

College students, like the rest of us, are operating with an impoverished worldview, what I call in my first book, *Gradual Awakening*, our *sickness of paradigm*. We live in a culture hell bent on materialism, hedonism, short-sightedness, Eurocentric hubris, and quick fixes, such as *McMindfulness*, a term I coined to capture the capitalist approach to marketing meditation, yoga, and spirituality. It is a culture whose very outlook is pathological in nature—the basis is a fundamental disconnection from, and an exploitation of, life's complex web of interdependence. With such a destructive foundation, many of its methodologies and educational approaches fail to address our mental health pandemic or our need for deeper meaning and connection.

College is also a critical time for development, a stage when young people transition to adulthood and face increased stressors in their lives. It would be an entirely appropriate juncture for a formal rite of passage, a Campbellian hero's journey, that would allow young folks to depart their familiar worlds, receive an initiation, and return to the world more confident and capable members of their broader communities. Sadly, modern materialist culture has lost touch with the mythos of initiation and the mythological perspective that would allow us to actually help our youth mature. As a result, students are left vulnerable to being unconsciously and involuntarily initiated by media, commercialism, and hyper competativeness, leaving them more narcissistic and self-involved, and less resilient and empathic, than when they started. While industrialized culture delays rather than facilitates development, our outdated educational model plays a role in disempowering youth by boxing them in endless results-oriented bureaucracies, fueled by hyperproductivity and mandated by the high priest of rationality. It doesn't have to be this way. To grow, students need wall-less classrooms and mindsets, fueled by creativity and wonder and mandated solely by the unique and sovereign divinity of each of their intuitions. We are due for a radical breakthrough, a disruption of the status quo. Schools, with a few important innovations, could be a place for holistic learning, an alchemical crucible for inspiring future altruistic leaders, if we are willing to complement book knowledge with emotional, interpersonal, and spiritual intelligence. This is what the Tibetan Buddhists call wisdom and what the Greeks called gnosis, creating an environment conducive for inner flourishing and well-being.

Academics as they stand now are not enough to combat our impoverished worldview or assist students in handling the pressures of modern living, of connecting with each other and the planet in a deeper, more meaningful manner. Meditation is a way of life that enables us to go beyond materialism, egocentrism, and satisfying every narcissistic impulse. It allows us to explore the depths and subtlety of consciousness, to regulate our emotions, to co-regulate and feel the inner worlds of others, and to discover a hidden treasure trove of meaning that comes from being generous, compassionate, and wisely responsible for maintaining balance in the delicate web of life. Meaning and purpose are universally derived from this inner process of discovery, which from time immemorial has been facilitated by many forms of introspection practices throughout ancient world cultures. Now that we have only scratched the surface and cracked the lid on contemplative practices in the West, the benefits of meditation have been scientifically studied and validated as a vehicle for greater well-being, improved cognitive functioning, optimal health, and other pro-social enhancements.

Fortunately for a whole new generation, this book skillfully lays the foundation for meditation to be embedded in higher education classrooms and clearly outlines various steps and approaches that have worked for practicing faculty. Much of the work has already been done for you. That said, I caution others to avoid stripped-down versions of meditation and other contemplative practices, ones that fail to acknowledge the deeper dimensions of spirituality. However, I believe new, integrative frameworks and deeply intentional approaches, such as the one provided in this book, will create opportunities for younger generations to be exposed to meditation within the context of their secular academic structures and schedules. Further, by incorporating the larger mythos underpinning meditation, rather than just the technique itself,

I think we will eventually build a bridge back to the Renaissance spirit that once valued multidimensional and interdisciplinary learning, aimed at enriching the soul, and incorporated rites of passage to help young people become whole and happy human beings.

I met Dr. Steve Haberlin when he participated in my Contemplative Studies program, which provides an in-depth study of the *lam rim,* or gradual path, in Tibetan Buddhism. Steve, a lifelong meditator, devoured the course material and completed the two-year program in just eight months, a testament to his dedication to remaining a student of lifelong learning. From our discourse, I could sense his passion and enthusiasm for contemplative practices, including different meditation methods such as mindfulness, loving-kindness, visualization, and breathwork, and wanting to understand their historical, cultural, and philosophical underpinnings. The research and work supporting this book resonate from that deeper framework of understanding and his years of experience practicing and teaching meditation methods.

This book provides academics (of all disciplines) with a compelling rationale for why meditation belongs in the college classroom, but it also presents a deep dive into the history of meditation and various techniques in a manner that both experienced meditators and faculty unfamiliar with meditative practices can grasp. The text is also packed with practical, specific techniques, tips, and steps to embed brief meditation into your classroom to help students with rising stress and distraction and to build a connected community of learners and altruistic leaders. In each chapter, Steve shares what he and his colleagues have learned over the years, including how to avoid pitfalls and errors when it comes to introducing meditation to your students, so you don't have to make those same mistakes. Finally, the book ends with spreading a culture of meditation across campus, which can assist in countering our frenzied, materialistic, goal-obsessed culture that adds to a pandemic of mental health.

This is a much-needed book during a critical sea change in history when our structures, from banking and economics to energy, ecology, and politics, are in transition. So too is education, a longstanding institution that must evolve with the times or risk contributing to the downfall of civilization by reducing our children to lifeless machines on a fast treadmill nowhere. It's high time a four-year college experience be reenvisioned as a classic hero's journey, a rite of passage that emboldens the nascent heroine to face her fear, find her treasure, and return to her tribe with a boon. Meditation as a technique is a noble first step in that direction; what will naturally follow is the philosophical ethos that will shift the paradigm from materialism back to spirit without sacrificing science. This book will open doors as it will change minds, allowing students to see themselves as they truly are: magnificent beings capable of radical change and deeply invested in shape-shifting a world for the benefit of all. Let this writing serve as a road map for that bright future, and with your help as a mentor, let's guide students back home to actualize their untapped potential.

Preface

My journey into meditation began at the age of 12. I began taking karate lessons at the local martial arts studio. The instructor, a no-nonsense man who always wore a Japanese-style bandanna (like Johnny Lawrence of the *Karate Kid* and *Cobra Kai* franchises), would instruct the class to sit on the ground with legs folded and "block out the noise" coming from the next-door aerobics studio (remember, this was the '80s).

As the walls reverberated with the sounds of *Flash Dance* music, I unsuccessfully tried like a maniac to concentrate and "meditate." I can't say I honestly enjoyed the experience, but I was intrigued.

In my early 20s, I formally learned Transcendental Meditation, which involves silently repeating a mantra, or sound, for 20 minutes twice a day. Immediately, I experienced a host of benefits, including stress reduction, more energy, mental clarity, and smoother relationships. I continued to practice Transcendental Meditation, occasionally joining group meditation sessions and attending a weekend retreat.

During this time, meditation and mindfulness were not mainstream or perhaps socially accepted the way they are today, and thus I would describe myself back then as a closet meditator. People gave me strange looks when they learned I meditated. So, often I would just tell them I was going to take a nap when I was really practicing Transcendental Meditation.

Thankfully, meditation, mindfulness, and yoga later gained steam, and schools in the United States began to experiment with the idea of incorporating these practices to help students. I jumped at this opportunity, and while working as an elementary teacher, I collaborated with a higher education colleague to teach contemplative practices to K–5 gifted students under my instruction. We shared meditation practices with the children and found promising results. I will never forget one child (let's call him "Bob"), who was diagnosed with attention deficit hyperactivity disorder, often stayed up all night playing video games, and was grouchy and restless the next day. After practicing meditation and yoga, Bob became so serene—and extremely focused. After engaging in an eating meditation activity, in which the students mindfully ate a marshmallow, he told us, "It felt like I had 1,000 marshmallows in my mouth!"

I continued to experiment with meditation and mindfulness within the context of the classroom, completing my doctoral dissertation on how these concepts impacted my instructional supervision of teacher candidates in elementary schools. At the same time, I felt the need to expand my meditation repertoire beyond Transcendental Meditation, so I joined a local Zen meditation group and began practicing *vipassana*. I furthered my studies of meditation through additional training and personal experience.

I never set out to teach meditation, but life seemed to take me in that direction. At the request of the college's provost, I established a meditation space on campus and organically began holding workshops and training in meditation for students, faculty, and staff. I have also been invited to train teachers in school districts located near the college. At the same time, I experimented with sharing meditation practices in my classroom and assisted other faculty in doing the same. During the past several years, I learned much about how to teach meditation—and just how challenging it can be. I have also seen firsthand the power of meditation and how it can help people.

My goal with this book is to simply share my experience and ideas that have worked for me and others regarding meditation in the college classroom. My wish is you find it meaningful, practical, and perhaps transformative.

Acknowledgments

First, I want to show deep, heartfelt appreciation for my spouse, Fon, who has relentlessly supported my academic career. You have been my biggest fan and my muse.

I would also like to thank my daughters, Marissa and Cassidy, for always believing in their dad and serving as shining examples of creativity and love.

I want to also strongly acknowledge faculty at Wesleyan College who courageously joined me in engaging in the Meditation in the Classroom project. Advancing my research and ideas—and this book—could not have happened without your support. Gratitude goes out to Suzanne Minarcine, Melanie Doherty, Brandi Simpson Miller, Deidra Donmoyer, Virginia Wilcox, Seth Selke, Laura Strausberg, and Tyler Schwaller.

In addition, I am very appreciative of how my work in meditation and mindfulness has been received at Wesleyan, and a special thanks to Provost Melody Blake: your constant support for all things meditation and mindfulness has really meant a lot.

A special thanks to the following colleagues willing to read and review drafts of this book and provide valuable feedback: Richard Brown, professor emeritus of contemplative education at Naropa University; Elizabeth Dorman, professor of teacher education, Fort Lewis College; and Cynthia Alby, professor of teacher education at Georgia College.

I must also acknowledge Miles Neale, Buddhist psychotherapist, teacher, author, speaker, and humanitarian. You have truly inspired me with your passion, commitment to learning, knowledge of Buddhism and meditation, caring for fellow contemplatives, and support.

Finally, I want to acknowledge the book's editor, Tom Koerner, and publisher, Rowman & Littlefield, for seeing the value in this work.

Chapter 1

Listen to the Bell!

THE ORIGINS OF MICRO-MEDITATION
IN THE COLLEGE CLASSROOM

Feeling a bit uneasy, the professor raised the Tibetan Singing Bowl, a small, metal bell struck by a wooden mallet, and said to the students: "Let's try to meditate together before we start class."

They looked at him strangely, like he had two, maybe three heads.

"Meditation could be a good way to start class, to clear our minds, reduce stress."

The professor rang the bell, and the students simply listened to it. Some closed their eyes. Some looked off, out the window, probably wishing they could get out of the room. The activity took only a few minutes—a *micro-meditation*. Then, class began. During the next class, he asked students to listen to the sound of the bell and then gently become aware of how their breath flowed in and out.

And that's how the Micro-Meditation project began.

From that moment, the professor began *every single class* at the small, private school, where he teaches in the teacher preparation program, with some form of meditation. Of course, the practice has become nuanced, but the essential elements are the same: take a comfortable position, listen to the sound, then follow the breath, witnessing it in its natural state.

MEDITATION IN THE COLLEGE CLASSROOM

I, the professor, later introduced meditation to undergraduate students, thinking it could help with the problems that my colleagues and I seemed to be facing: distracted, mentally drained students coming to class—a situation only exacerbated by the COVID-19 pandemic.

I was looking for a tool to help students transition to learning, something to help clear the headspace. The following is the protocol originally used (Haberlin, 2021).

First, wanting to be transparent, I explained that meditation was being used in more classrooms, including K–12 classrooms, to help students enhance focus, improve relationships, and de-stress. I mentioned research suggesting that meditation practice could help rewire the brain based on neuroplasticity (e.g., Creswell et al., 2007; Davidson et al., 2003; Hassed & Chambers, 2014), the strengthening the prefrontal cortex, which is responsible for cognitive functions, and the limbic system, responsible for emotional regulation.

During the first two weeks, I simply asked students to "focus their minds" on the sound of the Tibetan Singing Bowl, following it as it faded away, then "listen to what remains." Students meditated in seated positions and either closed their eyes or were encouraged to look downward. During week three, the meditation was extended slightly, as students were instructed to listen to the sound of the bowl, then "listen to their breath" or "follow their breath as it travels naturally in through the nostrils and out the nostrils." This practice was based on breath meditation, or what is known in the Buddhist tradition as *vipassana*. Each micro-meditation session lasted about three to four minutes.

The following academic year, the process was repeated with three classes (61 students); the results were published in the academic journal *College Teaching* (Haberlin, 2021). Overall, the students responded very favorably to engaging in brief meditations at the beginning of class. Here's what was found:

- Ninety-five percent reported experiencing states of calmness and stress reduction from practicing the micro-meditations.
- Eighty-eight percent perceived the meditation practice serving as a tool to help them refocus or reset mentally.
- Fifty-five percent viewed meditation as positively impacting the learning environment in the classroom.
- Six percent experienced difficulty with practicing meditation or reported no recognizable benefits.

While the data were preliminary, the results were encouraging. The experiment in implementing a tool to serve students as a bridge between the chaotic outside world, the classroom environment, and the mindset needed for learning seemed to be on track. For instance, one student wrote:

I started working and doing school full-time; I felt like the world was weighing on my shoulders. Every Monday after I had been in class all day, [course instructor's] class would calm me down with the bowl. When someone would use the bell at the beginning of class, I would feel my heart rate become normal instead of pumping fast. I would hear ringing in my ear even afterward, to help me remain calm. The bowl helped me through a lot this semester.

Another student stated:

One of the main things that I enjoy about starting class with meditation is that I am taking a moment to take a breather, not worry about all the million things that I must do—thats tend to stress me out sometimes. It is very relaxing to just focus on me and my needs instead of just work, work all the time. Being constantly on the go can be so exhausting sometimes because it just tends to wear you out so much!

The research also yielded insights into *how* to better introduce and teach students meditation in the classroom. For instance, the singing bowl often resonated well with students (no pun intended). It seemed to serve as a useful prop. The meditation practice didn't take long, just a few minutes, to have some impact. And the time was a wise investment—after meditation, students generally seemed more engaged, more focused.

EXPANDING MEDITATION ACROSS CAMPUS

However, this experience led to the question "How might this practice of micro-meditations work with other students on campus, in other programs, and with other professors?" Could a guide or framework be created that assisted higher education instructors in implementing this practice? For example, could there be a certain language that helps students feel comfortable? Could course instructors provide a more conducive setting in the classroom (e.g., by shutting the lights, closing the blinds)? Were there certain analogies and examples that would help students grasp the concept of meditation? When and what type of research around meditation should we share with students?

With such questions in mind, a faculty research team composed of eight professors interested in trying meditation with students was formed at the college. Some of them learned meditation during workshops held on campus. Others had practiced meditation on their own. The project consisted of asking students to engage in brief micro-meditations (witnessing the breath) before starting instruction. Team members were provided with a video model of students being guided through the meditation. A detailed guide was also provided via a Google Doc so the research team could add notes and questions. The team met monthly via (pandemic-friendly) Zoom to discuss experiences. In addition, students were surveyed anonymously throughout the semester in various classes to gauge their experiences and get feedback on the facilitation efforts.

Research findings echo some of the earlier discoveries. For example, most students participating in the project found meditating in class to be calming and pleasant, and it helped them focus. Wrote one student in a survey:

> My overall experience with learning and engaging in meditation in class is that it truly helps. I appreciate doing it because it gives me a moment to truly decompress from everything that I had to take care of before class. It really allows me to focus and put all my focus in class. It calms me down as well.

Of course, not every student embraced meditation (how to handle this will be discussed later in the book), like the student who wrote: "I skip it every day. I find it unnecessary."

MEDITATIVE INSIGHTS

Additionally, the research team discovered the following insights into how exactly to facilitate meditation in a way that works best for students:

- The singing bowl served as an effective prop, helping to calm students and giving them a point of focus.
- The vocal tone and delivery style of the instructor greatly mattered.
- Getting buy-in (their willigness to try meditation) from everyone or mostly everyone helped.
- Dimming the lights supported the activity.
- Closing their eyes assisted some students in relaxing.
- Creating a noise-free classroom environment was important; anticipating interruptions, such as students arriving late to class, needed to be considered.

Based on this feedback and their analysis, the team created a facilitation guide for meditation in the higher education classroom, which serves as the framework for this book. The guide covers everything from defining meditation for students, conceptualizing the practice and what happens to the mind using various metaphors and analogies, discussing the research and benefits, instructing students in actual techniques, to handling concerns, such as students who don't want to meditate or choose to refrain for religious/spiritual reasons. Each chapter in the book is structured around this guide.

WHAT TO EXPECT IN THIS BOOK

The remaining chapters of this book will unpack exactly what meditation is, summarize its history and lineage, and detail my work with colleagues in field-testing meditation practice with higher education students. The book also promises to provide a comprehensive guide to implementing brief meditation practices in your classroom, complete with specific tips, techniques, and examples. The following is a summary of each chapter.

Chapter 2: Why Meditation in the Higher Education Classroom?

This chapter makes the case of why college faulty should consider implementing brief meditation in the classroom. The discussion includes rising stress and anxiety rates among college students, and prevalent use of technology in the classroom and its impact on students' ability to focus and learn new content. A brief background on the contemplative movement (including the practice of meditation) in higher education classrooms is provided along with a conceptual framework for how meditation fits into academia and the educational system.

Chapter 3: What Is Meditation?

What exactly is meditation? How old is the practice? Where does it come from? This chapter serves as a basic overview of meditation. The chapter's content includes a brief history of meditation, an outline of various meditation traditions, and the benefits of practicing. The essential elements and principles of effective meditation, as well as common misconceptions, are also covered.

Chapter 4: Developing Your Meditation Practice (as a Stress-Out Academic?)

In this chapter, you will learn why and how, as an academic, you should start your own practice of meditation. Topics such as where to learn meditation, how to choose the right meditation for you, and where and when to practice are covered.

Chapter 5: Vipassana *and Other Meditation Methods for the College Classroom*

How do you actually teach meditation to students? What do you tell them to do when sitting? This chapter provides a comprehensive look at the practice of breath meditation, or *vipassana*, the main technique used with this facilitation framework. Several other meditation methods that are conducive to the college classroom are shared. Particulars, including body posture (in a classroom chair), witnessing the natural rhythm of the breath, and handling thoughts that come up, are explained.

Chapter 6: Introducing Students to Meditation

Where do you even start if you'd like to incorporate meditation in your classroom? This chapter unpacks how faculty and course instructors can introduce students to meditation in the classroom, including appropriate language to use to make them feel comfortable with the process, how to help students understand and conceptualize the practice, how to present the the rationale for meditation, including sharing research and benefits discovered through recent neuroscience, and helping students to culturally appreciate meditative traditions. I also address concerns about what to do if students do not want to meditate and how to provide alternative options.

Chapter 7: Setting the Stage for In-Class Meditation

How do you create the "right" conditions for students to meditate? How do you minimize distractions? Readers learn about how to create an ideal classroom environment for meditation and to deal with classroom distractions, such as cell phones and laptop computers. Other factors such as lighting and the use of a Tibetan Singing Bowl as a comforting "prop" are discussed. In addition, instructors learn how to establish the proper approach or attitude toward meditation (as one of being easy, playful, and relaxed).

Chapter 8: Advancing the Meditation

How do you keep the momentum going once students begin meditating? How do you keep it from getting routine? Readers learn how to continue the meditation practice in the classroom, building upon students' experiences and keeping it interesting. Examples of meditation "extensions," such as introducing different meditation techniques, walking meditation, and other mindfulness-based movement activities, are explained.

Chapter 9: The Meditation Facilitation Guide

What exactly should faculty say when guiding students through the practice? A comprehensive, field-tested faciliation guide for meditation in the college classroom is outlined, with complementary notes and guidance available for each section. Readers receive specific directions, with example scripts, on how to introduce meditation to students, instruct them in the practice, and continue the practice. The guide serves as a launchpad and framework for higher education faculty interested in trying out meditation in their classrooms.

Chapter 10: Spreading Meditation across Campus

How do you extend meditation across campus once students have bought into it? This chapter recaps the benefits of meditation in the higher education classroom and ways it might be implemented. Suggestions are provided for how to ingrain meditation practice into the fabric of the campus culture through faculty circles, research teams, and workshops for faculty and staff. Guidance on establishing a meditation space on campus is also addressed.

MAKING THIS GUIDE YOUR OWN

It's critical to note that the term "guide" was intentionally selected for the meditation facilitation protocol, as opposed to "script." While the document contains specific phrases and language that can be used, it is a guide and meant to aid faculty and lead you down the path, but the specific approach should be personalized and adjusted if necessary to meet the needs of your students and your teaching context. The guide serves as a launchpad, meaning you don't have to start from scratch if you want to implement meditation with your students. An effective guide, like one leading you through the Amazon or the Himalayas, is also familiar with the terrain, having traveled the path before. Thus, the guide steers you away from pitfalls and unnecessary obstacles and puts you in the proper direction.

Though this guide provides a track to run on, one also must remember that it was created using a certain map, a certain context, consisting of a particular group of students on a specific campus during a specific period in time. Therefore, you are encouraged to adjust information in the guide based on your experience and the individualized need of your students, classroom, and campus. While it's difficult to say what you might follow or adjust, perhaps you find that changing the order of how you present information might work better, or dropping certain phrases or metaphors is necessary. This will be part of your work, your adventure in bringing meditation into the classroom.

Sequencing of the Facilitation

The format of this book is intentionally sequenced in an order that likely best supports introducing meditation to your students. In this sense, the guide is a road map but also a recipe of sorts. Specific ingredients are mixed in a certain order to get results. While you might have the urge to jump around in the text, it's highly advised that readers interested in embedding meditation into the culture of their classrooms and curricula go through the chapters in the order they are presented.

For example, Chapters 2 and 3 provide the background and conceptual understanding necessary to share meditation with students. Chapter 4 encourages readers to *first* develop their own practice of meditation, while Chapter 5 gets into actual meditation techniques you can facilitate with students. The book addresses different entry points you can use to roll out meditation to students in Chapter 6, and Chapter 7 gives suggestions for setting the proper environment. In Chapter 8, readers will learn specifics on how to instruct students in brief meditation and keep the momentum going by implementing other meditation-related activities. All this leads to the actual meditation facilitation guide. Thus, each chapter builds upon the previous one, guiding you toward success based on what has been found to work in college classrooms.

CHAPTER SUMMARY

- This work, including the meditation facilitation guide, was developed in the field by real professors working with real college students. These ideas are based on what has worked and promising data.
- Despite all the information in this book, faculty planning to implement these ideas are highly encouraged to adjust the methods, techniques, and strategies to best serve their students' needs and classroom curricula.
- The book's format is intentionally organized so each chapter builds on the previous, providing the necessary background to utilize the facilitation guide.

Chapter 2

Why Meditation in the Higher Education Classroom?

Students are coming into your university or college classroom with higher stress and anxiety rates than ever before. With cell phones and other technological advances, they are more distracted than ever. The COVID-19 pandemic has only made a bad situation worse.

And you are expected to teach them.

This situation presents challenges never experienced in this particular way by faculty. Thus, new tools and approaches are needed. Perhaps embracing technology and current trends could help. On the other hand, maybe we need to turn to more ancient practices, including those that have been around for thousands of years.

It's time to expand our pedagogical toolbox. It's time to consider approaches that years ago might have seemed strange or exotic—or just plain crazy.

This book is about incorporating the age-old practice of meditation into the current higher education classroom as a device to help students focus, de-stress, connect, and center. The ideas in this book are based on years of research, practical implementation, and collaboration. In the end, the thesis of the book is this: *Meditation can become a powerful pedagogical tool, which like other approaches grounded in social-emotional learning and contemplative practices that get at the heart, has become a necessity.* This book goes beyond theorizing, though; it also provides a field-tested guide to get you started. Pausing to have meditation or "quiet" time—providing students with practical tools to de-stress, recenter, and focus *before* presenting content to them—makes perfect sense during this current age. Let's explore why.

SKYROCKETING STRESS AND ANXIETY RATES

College students appear to be more stressed and anxious now than at any time in recorded history. While more students are self-reporting mental illness due to a reduced stigma around the issue, there has been a major downward trend in students' resilience—or ability to cope with everyday stressors—and university counseling services are struggling to keep up with demands (Gray, 2015).

College students (between the ages of 18–29) fall into a stage of life known as the "emerging adult" (Arnett, 2000), which comes with its own unique challenges and stressors. They are in an intense period of identity development and growth and may feel tremendous pressure, as they must make choices that impact their future success and well-being. Higher education students find themselves in a transitory stage to young adulthood identified with academic pressures, isolation, homesickness, and financial pressures (Kadison and DiGeronimo, 2004; Mowbray et al., 2006). The inability to cope postively with these challenges leads to problems—namely, higher stress levels, which impact health and well-being (Vidic & Cherup, 2019).

In a report compiled by New York University, 55 percent of students nationally named academics as their biggest source of stress. Consequently, stress is the biggest impediment to academic performance, with six out of 10 college students reporting that they were so stressed they couldn't get their work done (American College Health Association, 2010; Dusselier et al., 2005; MtvU et al., 2009).

The pandemic—with disruptions to our way of life, swift changes from in-person classes to virtual teaching, and other disturbances—has made the situation worse. Due to COVID-19–associated disruptions, college students have experienced significant increases in stress, anxiety, depression, and suicidality (Clabaugh et al., 2021; Husky et al., 2020; Li et al., 2020; Luo et al., 2020; Patsali et al., 2020). Furthermore, female students report lower emotional well-being, and students of color reflected significantly higher levels of stress about their academic future compared with their white classmates (Clabaugh et al., 2021). The following studies shed more light on the problem:

- In an online survey by Active Minds of college students across the country, 80 percent reported that COVID-19 negatively impacted their mental health (Horn, 2020). Another nationwide survey reported similar results, with 85 percent of higher education students experiencing higher stress and anxiety rates (Blaisdell, 2020).

- A study of 195 university students found that many suffered from disturbed sleep, difficulty concentrating, and increased concerns about academic performance (Son et al., 2020).
- Another study of 2,000 undergraduate and graduate students from Texas A&M University reported the number of respondents expressing anxiety, depression, or suicidal thoughts was "alarming" (Wang et al., 2020).

Why does this matter in your college classroom? As stated, *stress is the biggest enemy to academic performance* (American College Health Association, 2016). The relationship between stress and poor academic performance has been well documented (e.g., Blumberg & Flaherty, 1985; Clark & Rieker, 1986; Linn & Zeppa, 1984, Struthers et al., 2000). Constant or chronic stress breaks down the brain's ability to function.

Over time, stress can have a shrinking effect on the prefrontal cortex, the part of the brain responsible for memory and learning. Neuroscience brain imaging shows that when the amygdala, a part of the brain in the limbic system that acts as a center for responding to fear and anxiety, is overactivated through stress, new sensory information cannot be passed through to parts of the brain associated with learning and memory. When this happens, students turn on an affective filter or enter an emotionally stressed state where they are no longer responsive to learning and new information. As Willis (2014) puts it, "if students are stressed, the information cannot get in" (n.p.). As Oman and colleagues note (2008), a vital developmental goal for college students is gaining the ability to manage excess or unwanted distress while facing healthy, appropriate challenges that enable them to grow.

TRAUMA IN HIGHER EDUCATION CLASSROOMS

Trauma has become more prevalent in our society. College-age students are particularly susceptible to experiencing trauma, which is defined as when a person's internal systems are unable to cope effectively with external stressors (Hoch et al., 2015). By the time students reach college age, 66 to 85 percent report having experienced a traumatic event (Read et al., 2011; Smyth et al., 2008). Up to 50 percent of college students are exposed to a potentially traumatizing event in the first year of college (Galatzer-Levy et al., 2012).

The negative impact of trauma on education and learning can stem back to elementary school years, with individuals experiencing cognitive loss and delays in physical, social, and emotional development that manifest in chronic absenteeism, grade repeating, and/or placement in special education (Shonk & Cicchetti, 2001). Higher education faculty are expected to be versed in trauma-informed pedagogy—for example, being able to notice and act on the signs of trauma in individual students. However, increased stress and trauma in academia are not the only "new" challenges we face as faculty.

DIGITALLY DISTRACTED

Across generations, we have become an "always on" society, connected yet in our own virtual world (Turkle, 2011). Due to technological advances, attention in society has become a "scarce resource and commodity." Constantly vying for our attention and targeting the psychic life, capitalist pursuits have created an overload on the senses, as "attention is increasingly experienced in a disjointed fashion" (O'Donnell, 2015, p. 190). Consequently, college students are not only more stressed out, but they are more distracted than ever. Like most people, college students are constantly bombarded by interruptions in the form of text messages, phone calls, television, and social media while performing other tasks (Delello et al., 2016). Consider the following:

- Driven by the need to socialize, college students, both male and female, have been addicted to cell-phone-related activities, namely social media sites (Roberts et al., 2014).
- A study of 935 undergraduate students found that the majority reported regularly multitasking, or engaging in two or more tasks simultaneously, and half admitted that this practice interfered with their ability to study (Mokhtari et al., 2015).
- Another study found that first-year college students multitasked significantly more than upper-class students (Delello et al., 2016).
- Studies suggest that technology usage such as text messaging negatively impacts classroom learning (Dietz & Henrich, 2014; Levine et al., 2013). For example, Internet addiction can affect college students' attendance, academic performance, and social skills (Hassan et al., 2021).

Mind Wandering in the Classroom

Long before the invention of the cell phone, educators have grappled with the concept of mind wandering and its possible negative impact on learning. Mind wandering is known as a "task unrelated thought that occurs when there is a shift away from external stimuli and representations associated with ongoing activities and goals" (Morrison et al., 2014, p. 1) In academic settings (such as your classroom), mind wandering can be particularly problematic when students are required to sustain their attention when learning course content—for example, during a lecture or class discussion.

In one study (Lindquist & McLean, 2011), college students in a psychology class were asked to report on how often they experienced mind wandering during three 50-minute lectures. Students' minds wandered throughout the class, with task-unrelated thoughts more likely to be reported (44 percent) than at the beginning of the class (25 percent)—which means attention worsened. Mind wandering also negatively impacted notetaking and retention of content. Thus, any methods or tools that might help students maintain focus and attention would be worth exploring.

THE NEED FOR NEW PEDAGOGICAL TOOLS AND SKILLS

Surveying 25 faculty members about the biggest change in culture at their university, Richard Light, a professor at Harvard Graduate School of Education, learned that most believed it was a renewed focus on teaching and experimenting with innovative methods in the classroom to better instruct students. Experiments to improve teaching involved three criteria: (1) the methods should not be too time-consuming; (2) methods should be inexpensive; and (3) improvements in students' learning should be measurable and clear. The spirit of this book echoes Light and Jegla's (2022) sentiments when they wrote:

> Any great university should constantly encourage its faculty to experiment with their classroom teaching. Most important, professors should commit (and be supported) to gathering reasonably rigorous evidence and data to see if their new teaching strategies are contributing to some tangible change in student learning. (n.p.).

Higher education faculty are facing a truly different audience, one that is more stressed out, more anxious, and more distracted. Clearly, new solutions and new tools are needed. Faculty must be more skilled in dealing with the mental and emotional challenges of students, and hone the ability to create supportive, calming, and enriching classroom environments. The ability to present content, assess learning, engage students in lively discussions, and design meaningful projects is essential in the teaching toolbox—but, due to changing times, they are not enough.

Sometimes, new tools don't surface as technological or creative inventions but rather require reaching back to the past to more ancient practices—in other words, applying ancient wisdom to modern problems.

The approach in this book meets the above criteria—implementing brief meditation in the classroom takes only a few minutes (once you get it established) and costs nothing (minus purchasing a bowl or chime if you choose). Measuring improvement in student learning (this includes social-emotional learning) could prove a bit harder, but you could assess results with students based on various factors (as faculty who have piloted this approach have done), including observational data, student surveys and written feedback, and student reflections. Of course, other research protocols could be designed.

THE PROMISE OF MEDITATION

Research on meditation has grown significantly in the last 30 years (Helber et al., 2012). While a comprehensive description and look at meditation will be provided in Chapter 3, research suggests that the practice of meditation hosts numerous physical and psychological benefits. For instance, meditation can make physical structural changes in the brain that produce beneficial effects (see, e.g., Creswell et al., 2007; Davidson et al., 2003; Hassed and Chambers, 2014; Lazar et al., 2005; and Wójcik et al., 2019), including:

- Better functioning
- Improved memory and concentration
- Stress reduction and resistance
- Lower anxiety
- Decreased depression
- Enhanced well-being
- Reduction of disorders (eating, substance abuse)
- Decreased chronic pain
- Increased compassion, nonjudgmental perspective

In some studies, various meditation practices produced structural changes in the brain, including those associated with learning and memory, impacting the density and volume of gray matter associated with various brain-related tasks (see Hölzel et al., 2008; Lazar et al., 2005; Pagnoni & Cekic, 2007; and Vestergaard-Poulsen et al., 2009). For example, Lazar and colleagues (2005) found that a non-control group, after just eight weeks of practice during a mindfulness-based stress reduction course, experienced thickening in the post cingulate, the area of the brain associated with wandering and self-relevance; the hippocampus, which is responsible for learning, memory, cognition, and emotional regulation; and the temporoparietal junction, which is connected to empathy and compassion. Conversely, meditation has been shown to shrink the amygdala, which houses the fear response mechanism in the brain and influences the body's fear, stress, and anxiety functions (Lagopolous et al., 2009).

THE MEDITATIVE MOVEMENT IN HIGHER EDUCATION

Contemplative practices, including meditation, have become more prominent in higher education (Coburn et al., 2011; Komjathy, 2017). Higher education faculty from various academic disciplines have been exploring the integration of meditation into curricula since the 1990s, prompting a movement known as "contemplative education" (Simmer-Brown & Grace, 2011). "Enterprising professors are now moving beyond that to integrate contemplative practices into the classroom, with the implicit goal of supporting a more transformative experience for students" (Brendel & Cornett-Murtada, 2019, p. 5; also see Zajonc, 2013).

Contemplative studies centers have been established at Naropa University, West Chester University, the University of Virginia, and Brown University. Contemplative practices, which include a variety of methods and techniques from various traditions, can include inviting students to engage in silence, visualization, labyrinth walking, contemplative art, deep listening, and storytelling, which can provide academic and social-emotional benefits in the classrooms. For instance, even done for short periods, contemplative practices can enhance attention, cognition, and cognitive flexibility (Jha et al., 2007; Tang et al., 2007; Zajonc, 2013; Zeidan et al., 2010). While often grouped within this larger umbrella of contemplative practices, meditation is not the same as contemplation. Meditation involves using different techniques or methods to go beyond the thinking mind—it involves mindfully noticing and letting go of thoughts and witnessing one's awareness. Contemplative practices, while meditative, can also involve thinking deeply or reflecting on thoughts and topics, or even prayer. While meditation usually involves stillness, contemplative practices are often embodied or artistic practices, such as yoga and brush stroke.

At the heart of these contemplative practices is "attentiveness to what one is trying to understand" and stabilizing "the wandering mind" (Owen-Smith, 2018, p. 26). Contemplative higher education scholars, including Arthur Zajonc, Peter Grossenbacher, Alexander Rossi, Daniel Barbezat, and Mirabai Bush, emphasize the importance of cultivation of attention, present-centered awareness, the development of the whole person in education, and fostering compassion and connection with others within the context of teaching and learning. These academics argue that contemplative practices, which rely on critical first-person inquiry of the nature of self and mind, are not in conflict with the more traditional, third-person approaches in the classroom but "rather complement, enrich, and expand these approaches" (Owen-Smith, 2018, p. 27).

The practice of meditation has been a central contemplative practice in higher education settings. Institutions such as New York University, the University of California San Diego, Columbia University, and the University of Washington now offer meditation training to help students deal with stress. Many of these colleges and universities have established designated spaces for meditation on campus (more on this in Chapter 10).

While research on meditation has grown significantly in the last 30 years (Helber et al., 2012), there have been relatively fewer studies around meditation and related contemplative methods in higher education curricula (e.g., Bush, 2013; Miller and Nozawa, 2002; Shapiro et al., 2011; and Tarrasch, 2015). Findings on college students and meditation in regard to stress reduction are consistent with studies on general adult populations (Walsh & Shapiro, 2006). However, research on meditation regarding the impact on academic learning and executive functioning among college students has shown mixed results (Chambers et al., 2008; Chan and Woollacott, 2007; Helber et al., 2012). For example:

- Hall (1999) studied 56 black undergraduate students in a psychology class and reported that those randomly assigned to a meditation group had higher grade-point averages.
- Another study found that when postsecondary students practiced a brief mindfulness meditation before a class lecture, retention levels of the information significantly increased (Chambers et al., 2008).
- A University of Kentucky study found that students who engaged in a 40-minute meditation demonstrated higher brain functioning than those opting to take a nap, read, or watch television (Kaul et al., 2010).
- However, a more recent study measured the possible impacts of higher education students doing mindfulness meditation for six minutes before class lectures and found no effects on academic achievement (Baranski & Was, 2019).

Mindfulness meditation seems to tame the wandering mind (Brewer et al., 2011; Mrazek et al., 2013). In a study by Morrison and colleagues (2014), university students reported enhanced sustained attention and lower mind wandering after just seven weeks of mindfulness meditation.

In regard to helping college students deal with stress, meditation seems to help. Oman and colleagues (2008) tested students' stress levels and found that those taught a mindfulness meditation technique had significantly decreased stress levels after eight weeks of practice. Tarrasch's (2015) research on introducing counseling and special education graduate students to meditation showed promising results, including students reporting more awareness of their thoughts and actions, feeling calmer and better able to cope with stress, and enhanced relationships, though many described challenges with maintaining the practice, especially when first beginning.

Grace (2011), who has incorporated meditation in the college classroom at the University of Redlands, discovered that the practice helped students sharpen their habits of mind and enjoy mental evenness in the face of everyday turmoil. As one student reflected: "Meditation made me feel completely revitalized. I had to write a paper after our class, and I noticed how quickly and confidently I did it. . . . My mind was always wandering. I am now able to focus" (p. 242).

My research and that with colleagues (Haberlin, 2021; Haberlin et al., 2022) suggest that when it comes to helping students de-stress, focus, and transition into learning when coming to class, meditation certainly helps most students. A student described it this way:

> One of the main things that I enjoy about starting class with meditation is that I am taking a moment to take a breather, not worry about all the million things that I must do—that tends to stress me out sometimes. It is very relaxing to just focus on me and my needs instead of just work, work all the time. Being constantly on the go can be so exhausting sometimes because it just tends to wear you out so much!

While research connecting meditation to resilience is still emerging, studies suggest that mindfulness-based activities, including sitting meditation, can benefit students experiencing trauma (Davidson, 2017). For example, Kuhl and Boyraz (2017) found that trauma-exposed college students scoring higher on mindfulness scales had more trust in others and perceived higher levels of social support.

In a review of 18 mindfulness meditation studies with college students, Bamber and Schneider (2020) found numerous benefits. First, all of the studies showed that college students engaging in mindfulness meditation intervention (similar to those being promoted for the classroom in this book) experienced increased awareness, being more present in the here and now. "Through meditative practice students became aware of their countless thoughts and sensations and found they were able to gain control over these thoughts" (p. 18).

In all of the studies, researchers also noted that students were better able to regulate emotions and experienced increased coping ability. "Students were able to use that awareness to refocus their attention to the task at hand or eliminate the perceived stress before it became overwhelming" (p. 19).

In 11 of the studies, students reported that meditation impacted their relationships, including promoting greater social connection. Finally, students spoke of less perceived anxiety, increased focus, and greater work productivity. Also, "they were more relaxed and less anxious during testing which allowed them to be 'more careful and thorough on tests'" (p. 20). In the end, meditation practices show much promise for helping college students deal with ever-increasing levels of stress and anxiety.

A CONCEPTUAL FRAMEWORK FOR MEDITATION IN THE CLASSROOM: TWO WINGS OF A BIRD

When implementing meditation in the college classroom, a conceptual framework can provide an overall structure and prompt faculty to reflect on their pedagogical values and beliefs. For instance, *what do you believe about education, about learning, about teaching? How do you view various educational theories and models, including the traditional or prevalent approaches to teaching and learning in higher education?*

When debating if meditation has a place in the college classroom, consider this rationale: Higher education curricula are incomplete in the general sense. Academia, as the name indicates, is intensely focused on academics. Students declare majors and study specific disciplines and fields, acquiring the knowledge and skills to enter those fields and the workplace. In other words, they learn to make a living. However, if we think of education as the Latin word suggests, to draw out and awaken inherent potential, then the system falls short. Conventional academic teaching aims only for students to "think about" rather than to "know within" (Simmer-Brown & Grace, 2011).

Promoting meditation and other contemplative practices in the higher education classroom, academics such as Zajonc (2013) have called for a revolution in higher education teaching, "an epistemology of love that embodies and practices respect, gentleness, intimacy, vulnerability, participation, transformation, the formation of new capacities, and the practice of insight" (p. 91).

A complete or more holistic education provides students with opportunities to develop awareness—become more conscious, more emotionally intelligent, more in tune with themselves, others, and the environment—to know the powers of their minds, and to know themselves. Education must be more than that pouring in; it must include deepening and widening the well. Thus, if academics are one wing, meditation is the other wing needed for students to discover and unfold their inner potential—to not only make a living but to live fully.

Embedding meditation in the college curriculum can help students go beyond learning to critically thinking about and also better understanding the thought process itself and how emotions arise in the mind. They can learn to become more centered in their thinking, rather than being tossed about like a leaf in the wind, falling whim to any thought or emotion that arises in their daily lives.

Becoming more mindful through meditative practices can provide students with "recognition and choice" (Miles, 2011)—providing the space for them to be empowered to make conscious choices rather than fall prey to habitual reactivity.

Advances in neuroscience are showing the dangers of neglecting the inner life of the individual. As Simmer-Brown and Grace (2011) note, "scientific studies of contemplatives have demonstrated that the meditative mind achieves states of concentration, attention, awareness, creativity, happiness, well-being, and compassion for others more frequently and more powerfully than the non-contemplative mind" (p. xv).

SILENCE AND PAUSE: THE MISSING INGREDIENTS IN COLLEGE CLASSROOMS

College classrooms have become synonymous with speed, busyness, and the cramming of information. This educational environment echoes the outside society. "We are a culture that fears silence and one that is far more comfortable with noise" (Owen-Smith, 2018, p. 29). Some faculty may view silence or brief pauses in the classroom as failure to teach or impart knowledge, as a waste of time; however, periods of communal silence—which can involve simply sitting quietly or listening to a meditation bell at the start of class—can be a powerful teaching tool that allows creative insights to emerge, for deeper reflection to occur, and for the mind to recharge.

Early research suggests that silence in the classroom can enhance mental clarity and help individuals differentiate between important and unimportant stimuli (Hart, 2009; Prochnik, 2011). As Miller (1994) posits, silence and meditation practice are integrally linked. Brief meditation—for instance, prior to academic instruction—intentionally provides students with gaps of silence. It directly buffers against our fast-paced, information-packed, busy classroom culture.

MEDITATION AS A PEDAGOGICAL TOOL

This is not to say that meditation in the college classroom is a silver bullet; that is not the message of this book. Rather, brief meditation practice can be seen as another pedagogical tool, one that assists with cognitive and social-emotional challenges that students face. Meditation might be seen as another method for building a learning community and creating the supportive, open, safe environment needed for learning to occur. In addition, meditation can serve as a much-needed attention bridge or transitioning tool for students coming in from their busy, digitally distracted world to the classroom or the virtual format, where they are expected to think, learn new content, and engage in meaningful discussions.

While studies suggest that meditation is a useful intervention for college students, little attention has been placed on how to effectively teach meditation to this population, which can be resistant to engaging in such practices. "Students are often skeptical of mindfulness meditation and may worry it is too 'new-agey' or 'touchy-feely'" (Rogers, 2013, p. 547). Feeling pressed for time, college students might feel overburdened, making it difficult to sell them on the benefits of meditation. This book sheds much light on how to introduce and teach meditation to college students. By embedding brief meditation activities into the classroom, it eliminates the argument from students that they don't have time. This work also addresses how to handle resistance from students who don't want to engage in meditation.

THE MEDITATIVE CLASSROOM JOURNEY

Implementing any new pedagogy can be nervewracking; you never know exactly how students will respond. The same might go for asking students to meditate. One thing is for sure: Our higher education teaching practices must evolve with the times to accommodate new challenges and demands. We must do something different if we are to address the rising stress and anxiety rates of students sitting in our classrooms, along with the inability of society to focus and be in an optimal state for learning new information and gaining skills.

The Three Barriers to Pedagogical Change (and How This Book Can Help)

The most commonly cited barriers to pedagogical change among faculty are insufficient training, time, and incentives (Brownell & Tanner, 2012; Henderson et al., 2010). Let's take a brief look at each concern within the context of implementing meditation in the classroom.

Lack of Training

Faculty often cite that they don't feel equipped to teach, and thus want formal training before trying to change the way they teach. This is understandable. One needs working knowledge before making a change. This book provides practical knowledge for embedding brief meditation in the college classroom, knowledge that is based on the experience of other faculty innovating in the same way. This book, along with the meditation facilitation guide, is more than enough to get started on inviting students to meditate for a few minutes prior to academic instruction. Of course, while this book gives detailed instructions, it would be helpful to seek additional information and training in the area of meditation and to gain experience, if you feel that is necessary. But remember, faculty working on the Meditation in the Classroom project had less training and knowledge than you will have when you finish reading this book, and they reported an overall positive experience and beneficial results.

Time

The second barrier to changing teaching is not having enough time. Again, this is completely understandable as faculty wear many hats and are often pressed for time. The good news with this pedagogical tool is, after introducing meditation to students and laying the groundwork, it takes just a few minutes each class. To put it in numbers, a faculty member teaching two classes per week during a 16-week semester would spend just 96 minutes on this teaching strategy (assuming the meditation lasts no longer than three minutes per class). That is a small investment for the benefits and gains you could see with your teaching and students.

Incentives

Finally, the third barrier is wondering whether the new teaching method is worth it. Will you see a payoff? This book provides examples—quotes from real students and professors—about the power and possible impact of meditation in the classroom. Another question to ask yourself: *Is your present approach to creating a positive, supporting environment and preparing students to learn and master new content (in spite of their stressed states) working?* If not, it's time to try something new.

This book will hopefully ease these concerns and others by outlining an approach for embedding meditation into your existing classroom routines and practices—not replacing what you already do, but rather supplementing it. The experiences and guidance shared in this book can help reduce the learning curve and anxiety that come from trying new techniques with students. Who knows, perhaps you will also experience greater states of clarity, calm, creativity, and focus as you discover meditation and what it can do for both you and your students. Let's get started.

CHAPTER SUMMARY

- College students are more stressed, anxious, and distracted than ever. Trauma has become more prevalent on university and college campuses. This scenario presents more challenges to teaching.
- Faculty must explore innovative strategies and develop new skills to deal with these challenges.
- Meditation demonstrates promising benefits, including in the college classroom. Implementing brief meditation into classes can become another effective pedagogical tool.

Chapter 3

What Is Meditation?

WHAT EXACTLY IS "MEDITATION"?

The word "meditation" has been used in many ways. The Sanskrit word *dhyana* has been translated to mean the process of meditating or training the mind through contemplation. Meditation has also been associated with the Tibetan word *gom*, which means "to become familiar," as in to know the mind. Currently, meditation is used as a generic term for practicing various methods of calming the mind and dealing with stress. However, over time, the word has become convoluted, misinterpreted, and conflated with other words. For instance, the word "meditation" comes from the Latin term *meditatum*, which means to "ponder." In the West, meditation has also been described as thinking deeply about something, as in, "I'm going to meditate on this." That's not at all what we are talking about here regarding having students engaged in meditation in the college classroom.

For the purpose of this book, meditation is essentially a state of non-doing—no mental or physical activity. One drops all doing and experiences being. You simply *are*. When meditating, one reaches a relaxed, open state of awareness. As Shumsky (2001) explains it, "your mind settles to tranquility, and your body becomes still. Your body is more relaxed, often more deeply than sleep, yet your mind is more alert than wakefulness. Your awareness expands" (n.p.).

Meditation is a state of no content beyond the ordinary thinking mind. Furthermore, meditation has been described as one's natural state, which has been lost due to conditioning and society. Like a diamond covered with dust, this state is not something to gain or achieve but rather something to rediscover.

You might have inadvertently entered a meditative state during your daily activities or experiences. For example, while watching a sunset, you might have become fully immersed in the present, just sitting and observing the beauty of nature. Your body completely relaxed, coming to your "center," your mind free of the constant chatter. You didn't evaluate the experience but rather lived it and enjoyed it fully. You had a meditative moment.

Meditation is also a synchronicity or unity between mind, body, and consciousness. Some might have experienced this state (sometimes called "the zone" in sports) when running or maybe surfing, when one's energies are totally in rhythm with a wave. The mind is devoid of thought and chatter, just pure awareness. Others might have fallen into meditation when falling in love or experiencing a first kiss—one is totally immersed in the moment; nothing else matters.

Meditation master Osho (1977) defines meditation in the following manner: "Meditation is a state of silence. Meditation is a state of no desire; meditation is a state of no past, no future. . . . Meditation is a state of not trying for anything, not even meditation. Meditation is a state of nonstriving, utter relaxation. The sheer joy of being is what meditation is" (p. 5).

More modern definitions of meditation have been attempted. Using both traditional and clinical parameters, Cardoso et al. (2004) created an operational definition, positing that to be considered meditation, it must fit the following criteria: (1) utilize a clearly defined, specific technique, (2) involve muscle relaxation somewhere during the process, (3) be logic relaxation (i.e., not intending to judge or analyze), (4) be a self-induced state, and (5) use a self-focus skill, anchor, or reference point for attention.

Of course, as Cardoso and colleagues acknowledge, this definition excludes active meditation techniques, such as Dynamic Meditation, which involves moving about, jumping, and chanting before sitting quietly, and other forms of activity where meditation might occur (for instance, while walking or running).

Interestingly, the word "meditation" has the same root meaning as "medicine" and "median." Meditation is medicinal in the sense that it removes mental afflictions—for example, the constant chatter of the mind and emotions such as fear and anxiety. It is a deconstructive process that brings one to the natural state of the mind, the vast, open awareness and clarity that has been lost to mental and social conditioning. As Singh (2014) writes, the practice of meditation "frees us from our persistent automatic thought patterns" and frees our minds "from the constraints of years of mental conditioning and inner conflicts" (p. 2). Meditation is also a kind of psychological centering; one's energy or awareness is no longer scattered or pulled in various directions by life.

As neurologist and long-time Zen Buddhist James Austin (1998) explains, "meditation helps us retreat from all the wheels going around. It relieves us from self-inflicted trains of thought, trains driven by and loaded with the fossil fuel of ancient emotions" (p. 12).

Finally, a brief note on the difference between *meditation* and *mindfulness*. While these two terms are sometimes used interchangeably, meditation is a state of deeper awareness reached through various techniques and methods; mindfulness is the quality of being present and aware. The quality of mindfulness might be used to support a specific meditation method, such as breath meditation, or *vipassana*. *It helps to consider mindfulness as a quality while meditation is a practice.*

WHERE DID MEDITATION ORIGINATE?

The practice of meditation can be found in cultures and traditions around the world throughout history. Providing an exact timeline and history of meditative practices is no easy task, as information and accounts vary. We do know that meditation goes back thousands of years. To introduce meditation in the classroom, instructors do not need to become meditation historians but should develop an overall, healthy appreciation of meditation traditions.

It's difficult to say how long meditation has existed and who exactly developed the first meditative techniques. Scholars speculate that meditation "might be as old as humanity itself" based on the potential meditative capacities of Neanderthals (Meade, 2019, n.p.). Some of the oldest accounts of meditation appear in early written records in India around 1500 BCE. Mentions of meditation can also be found in earlier Chinese Daoist writings dating back to the third century BC.

The intent of this book is not to provide a comprehensive look at various meditation traditions and approaches, but rather to offer a cultural appreciation of where meditation techniques were developed, refined, and used. For example, many of the methods presented in this book and embedded within the facilitation guide are grounded in Buddhism but have been practiced in the United States for decades.

Vedic Tradition

In the ancient Vedic civilization in India, thousands of years ago meditation masters experimented with methods to explore consciousness. This knowledge, or *Vedi*, was passed down orally and later committed to writing. Transcendental Meditation, made popular by the Beatles and advocated by celebrities today, was developed by Maharishi Mahesh Yogi in the Vedic tradition.

Chapter 3

Yoga

In the Hindu tradition, yogis have practiced forms of meditation. Even today in the West, where Hatha yoga is popular, with physical postures and stretches, sessions often end with lying or sitting meditation.

Buddhism

Perhaps meditation is most often associated with Buddhism, developed 26 centuries ago. While it's sometimes mistakenly believed that the Buddha invented meditation, he learned techniques from Vedic masters of his time and developed his own techniques (Meade, 2019). Various meditative methods have since emerged from the different traditions of Buddhism.

Sufism

Within this ancient Islamic tradition, which dates back some 1,400 years ago, different meditative techniques are used, including the use of mantras and breath. Sufis also practice a moving meditation, known as whirling, in which they twirl around continuously while maintaining their psychic center.

Christianity

Translations of the word "meditate" are found in the Bible. Christian meditation, while not the same practice as meditation described in this book, involves filling the mind with scripture. One such practice, *Lectio Divina*, or "divine reading," involves reading verses of scripture and reflecting and praying on them (Reyes, 2020).

A BRIEF HISTORY OF MEDITATION IN THE WEST

Early interest in meditation surfaced in the West in the 1700s when Eastern philosophy texts mentioning meditation techniques and practices, including *The Upanishads, The Bhagavad Gita,* and *The Buddhist Sutras,* were translated into different European languages.

The concept of meditation was referenced during the late 1800s by philosophers, including Voltaire and Schopenhauer. Meditation became recognized in the United States in the 20th century, after yogi Swami Vivekananda presented at the Parliament of Religions in Chicago (Meade, 2019). A number of spiritual teachers from India later migrated to the United States to spread their teachings, including Swami Rama from the Himalayan Institute, Paramahansa

Yogananda from the Self-Realization Fellowship, and Maharishi Mahesh Yogi, who taught Transcendental Meditation.

Buddhist masters who escaped during the Chinese invasion of Tibet, including Chungyam Trungpa, who arrived in the United States in 1970 teaching meditation and established Naropa University in Boulder, Colorado, and Shunryu Suzuki, who established the San Francisco Zen Center in the early 1960s, also helped popularize meditation practice.

Meditation continued to gain steam in the West into the 1970s as scientific research was being conducted on the topic. In 1997, the American Psychological Association formally acknowledged meditation, stating that "meditation may facilitate the psychotherapeutic process" and encouraging research into its usefulness (Kutz et al., 1985).

After learning meditation while studying at MIT, Jon Kabat-Zinn created the Mindfulness-Based Stress Reduction program in 1979 at the University of Massachusetts Medical School, further popularizing and helping to mainstream contemplative practices in the West.

Deepak Chopra, a former student of Maharishi, further promoted meditation through dozens of best-selling books. Celebrities also openly embraced various meditation techniques, including Transcendental Meditation, helping to further spread its popularity. Today, there's an estimated 2,400 meditation centers across the country, with programs and practices being infused into schools, hospitals, businesses, and other secular settings.

WHY PRACTICE MEDITATION?

Meditation is needed more than ever to handle the current pace of life and amount of information. The average person consumes about 34 gigabytes of data each day, an increase of 350 percent over the last three decades, through social media, television, radio, video games, and text messaging (Bilton, 2019). This includes students in your classroom.

Technological advances seem to be shortening the ability to focus. With so many more options for distraction, including playing music, connecting with friends, and playing games on our cell phones, we can't pay attention as well. One study found that the average attention span decreased by four seconds, from 12 to eight, which is shorter than that of a goldfish (Walden University, n.d.).

People, including our students (and maybe yourself), are also more stressed than ever. As a result of the COVID-19 pandemic—compounded by pervading societal pressures, including mass shootings and climate change—individuals experienced increased stress levels (American Psychological Association, 2020). Despite all our technological advances and apparent conveniences, society does not seem to be happier or more satisfied, as individuals are plagued by sleep disorders, anxiety, depression, drug and alcohol abuse, and other stress-related problems. As Jacobs (2003) keenly notes in this book *The Ancestral Mind*, "one of the great ironies of modern life is that, despite the new global connectedness brought about by the telecommunications revolution, we feel increasingly *disconnected* from ourselves, from others, and from our world" (p. 4).

Meditation is a vehicle to connect with one's inner world that provides a means for inner transformation (Ricard, 2010), a way to live more sanely in what seems to be an insane world. The practice of meditation can provide a way to provide a gap between what is happening and how one responds. It will not necessarily change the outside world but rather how you experience it. This space or gap creates the conditions for what Buddhist psychotherapist Miles Neale (2017) calls "recognition and choice" (p. 18)—the ability to recognize what is occurring and respond in a new or more favorable way, thus breaking the habitual patterns of reactivity that are causing stress and anxiety.

Where's the Proof?

Research on the benefits of meditation has vastly increased due to advances in neuroscience. For example, the number of scientific articles on meditation has grown from about 500 in 1990 to more than 4,000 (Vieten et al., 2018). However, we still don't know everything about meditation and what it can do for us. Meditation studies have been criticized for a lack of methodological quality (Ospina, 2007), making it difficult to draw hard conclusions. Researchers know little about how effects such as changes in brain tissue, metabolism, and the immune system vary from person to person and why this is the case (Fessenden, 2015). Nevertheless, this intensified interest in scientific research on meditation has shown that various meditation techniques can yield a host of possible mental and physical benefits.

Meditation's Impact on Stress

In a meta-analysis of studies conducted on meditation's impact on cortisol, a stress hormone, researchers found a significant benefit of meditation interventions on cortisol levels in blood samples (Koncz et al., 2021). In one of the studies, veterans with post-traumatic stress disorder showed significant positive changes in cortisol levels after four weeks of mindfulness meditation (Bergen-Cico et al., 2014). In a separate study of 271 distressed survivors of breast cancer, participants displayed lower cortisol levels after learning mindfulness meditation (Carlson et al., 2013).

Another indicator of stress is low skin resistance. Meditators, particularly those practicing Transcendental Meditation, have reflected high skin resistance during studies (Bagga & Gandhi, 1983; Bono, 2017).

Meditation's Psychological Impact

Meditation practice—in particular, mindfulness meditation methods—can produce positive psychological impacts (Eberth & Sedlmeier, 2012). Intensive meditation practice can result in enhanced levels of mindfulness, significantly reduced depressive symptoms, reflective rumination, and negative affect, and improvement in executive functioning (Chambers et al., 2008). Below are some other findings related to the psychological effects experienced by meditators:

- Meditators may experience enhanced visual sensitivity and visual imagery abilities (see, e.g., Brown et al., 1984a, 1984b; Heil, 1983; Keithler 1981; and Linden, 1973).
- Transcendental Meditation practitioners demonstrated higher performance on nonverbal intelligence tests (Jedrczak et al., 1986), and regular practice of the technique suggested higher school grades and learning ability and improved memory (Cranson et al., 1991).

Meditation's Effect on Health

Meditation is now widely accepted as a viable method for maintaining health and wellness (Horowitz, 2010). In medical settings, meditation has been shown to be an effective therapy for treating various conditions and the psychological effects that accompany chronic illness and pain. For example, research shows regular meditation may help strengthen the immune system. One study investigated the impact of healthy employees who were all vaccinated against influenza (Davidson, 2003). Researchers found significant increases of activation on the left side of the brain's frontal context, which is an area associated with positive emotion, and significant increases in markers of antibodies for the flu vaccine among meditators compared to the control group. Here are some other health benefits associated with meditation:

- Studies indicate that meditation can slow heart rates and lower blood pressure for individuals who are low or moderately hypertensive (Tamini, 1975; Bono, 1984; Sears & Raeburn, 1980; Swami Karmananda Saraswati, 1982; Wallace et al., 1983).
- Meditative interventions have proved beneficial for other clinical conditions, including cardiovascular disorders, pain syndromes and

musculoskeletal diseases, respiratory disorders such as asthma and congestive obstructive pulmonary disease, dermatological problems such as psoriasis, allergies, and immunological disorders (see Hussain & Bhushan, 2010).

MEDITATION AND NEUROPLASTICITY

Meditation has been associated with the phenomenon of neuroplasticity, the brain's ability to adapt and rewire itself based experience, as in the case of Lazar and colleagues' (2005) research where after eight weeks of mindfulness-based meditation training, participants' brains showed structural changes. For much of the 20th century, it was believed that the adult brain did not change, that the adult mammalian brain in general remained stable over the course of its lifetime. Advances in brain scanning and neuroimaging technologies changed scientists' minds over this matter. While the research is not conclusive, several studies imply that various meditation methods can in fact change the long-term structure and function of the brain.

For instance, in one study researchers examined differences in Tibetan monks and novice meditators in their responses to adverse sounds (Brefczynski-Lewis et al., 2007). The monks demonstrated increased activation in the anterior insular of the brain when hearing adverse noise as opposed to positive sounds. The research suggests that meditation practice may have created structural changes resulting in the increased ability to regulate emotional reactivity.

HOW MEDITATION WORKS

Meditation allows one to become more familiar with how the mind works. When meditating, the meditator is turning their attention 180 degrees inward, exploring his or her inner landscape. Typically, an individual's attention is focused outward on the physical environment. Meditative techniques focus on new dimensions through becoming more aware of the body and its sensations, the breath, and/or the workings of the mind—for instance, how thoughts bubble, how emotions arise, or how memories surface. In essence, the meditator gains clarity of their mental processes. As one meditator told *The Atlantic*, "Mindfulness meditation is not a nice little thing. It's not like frosting on a cupcake. This is a *major* transformation" (Kulze, 2013, n.p.).

In addition, meditation is a "jump into the unconscious" (Rajneesh, 1976, p. xvi). The practice involves transcending the conscious mind, exploring typically unchartered aspects of consciousness. For instance, during

Transcendental Meditation, in which the meditator silently and effortlessly recites a mantra or sound, the meditator experiences subtler and subtler levels of conscious thought, finally arriving at the source of thought and the fourth state of consciousness (Domash, 1975; Travis et al., 2011).

Lin and Parikh (2019) have a unique explanation for how meditation powerfully transforms. Drawing on quantum physics, they assert that there's no real separation between the subjective and objective world, and everything, all matter, is made up of particles and energy. Thus, "the energy and intention of our minds may be invisible, but when we enter a meditative mode, we can tap into the intangible, energetic-like reality, and we get into touch with deeper levels of our existence" (p. 9). In other words, we can experience inner transformation or change at the level of our awareness, in our consciousness, through meditation.

Science has caught up with this idea, as meditators show actual structural changes in the brain as a result of practice. From a neuroscientific standpoint, meditation operates through a combination of mechanisms: attention regulation, emotion regulation, bodily awareness, and a change of perspective on the self. These mechanisms "work synergistically, establishing a process of enhanced self-regulation" (Hölzel et al., 2011, p. 537).

MEDITATION AND "NO-MIND"

To conceptually understand meditation, it's necessary to grasp the concept of "no-mind," known in Japanese as *mushin*. Used within the Zen Buddhism context, no-mind is not mindlessness or devoid of intelligence but rather a state of pure consciousness beyond the ordinary thinking mind. No-mind is the goal (if there is one) of meditation. No-mind is a state of mind that is clear, open, and free from outside distractions. As Belshee (2005) writes, "No Mind is a meditative state in which the practitioner leaves behind all the dreck in his life, allowing himself to just be" (n.p.). No-mind is the experience of being immersed in the moment. Austin (1998) explains that no-mind is "not complete mental blankness, as if one were asleep. But rather it represents freedom from thought pollution" (p. 57).

Meditators may enjoy glimpses of no-mind, brief periods when thinking seems to cease and time doesn't seem to exist. One is no longer self-conscious but rather experiencing a state of expanded awareness. A helpful illustration of no-mind in action can be found in the 2003 film *The Last Samurai*, in which actor Tom Cruise plays a disenchanted ex-U.S. army captain during the American Indian Wars who embraces the ways of the Japanese warriors, the *samurai*. During one scene, Cruise is instructed to trust no-mind when practicing his martial arts skills, to let go of his conscious thinking about how to swing his sword and anticipate his opponent's moves and about his worries of what onlookers might think (https://www.youtube.com/watch?v=-DAWlspPiuI&t=36s).

A PEAK INSIDE THE MEDITATOR'S MIND

By the 1960s, advances in electronic instrumentation enabled researchers to measure brain waves, heart rate, and other physiological data, giving us a glimpse into the mind of the meditator. Herbert Benson, a Harvard Medical School cardiologist, performed extensive research on Transcendental Meditation and what he later called the Relaxation Response, a similar technique. His findings give a glimpse into the brain during meditation, particularly within the context of slowing the conscious, thinking mind (the frontal cortex) and producing mental states associated with creativity, relaxation, and decreased reactivity.

When meditating, our brain waves slow down, as measured by decreased beta activity. Beta waves are alertness waves and the most active, measuring 15 to 40 cycles a second. A person who is deeply engrossed in a conversation, debating, or teaching content would be experiencing high beta activity (Jacobs, 2003).

As the person continues to meditate, alpha activity generally rises. Alpha waves, which range from nine to 14 cycles per second, represent a non-arousal state. Alpha occurs when reflecting, resting after work, or walking through a garden (Herrmann, 1997). This is followed by increases of theta waves, which are even slower in frequency, registering five to eight cycles a second. A person experiencing a theta state might be daydreaming, running outside, relaxing in the tub, or experiencing a flow of creative ideas. It is a very positive mental state.

Research suggests that extended practice enhances the intensity and duration of less-aroused states—for instance, experienced meditators showed greater increases in theta activity. The significance of these findings demonstrates that regular practice of meditation activates healthier, more efficient aspects of the brain and diminishes the harmful ones. As Jacobs (2003) notes, "the appearance of slower brain wave patterns like theta waves indicates that the reticular formation and thalamus are reducing the arousal level of the cortex so that the cortex can relax, take a break from its normal processing of information and conserve energy" (p. 129). Consider this information within the context of the college classroom and how assisting students to access such states of mind could benefit their well-being and learning—to slow the business of their brains—and it becomes powerful and inspiring.

CATEGORIZING MEDITATION TECHNIQUES

Scholars have struggled to define and classify various meditation techniques. Generally, meditation methods have been codified into three types: (1) concentrative, (2) analytical, and (3) visualization. A concentrative technique could involve gently focusing on the breath or a mantra. An analytical meditation might require studying a text or a principle, such as *impermanence* in the Buddhist tradition, then deeply reflecting it. A visualization meditation could involve picturing a spiritual teacher, such as the Buddha or Jesus, and imagining to embody their qualities.

Generally, researchers have divided meditative techniques based on whether they are considered more focus-attention oriented or based on open awareness. Matko and Sedlmeier (2019) have more recently proposed a empirically derived classification system for meditation techniques. Based on the amount of body orientation in the method and the level of activation, they have created seven main categories of meditation techniques: (1) body-centered meditation, (2) mindful observation, (3) contemplation, (4) mantra meditation, (5) visual concentration, (6) affect-centered meditation, and (7) meditation with movement.

THE FUNDAMENTALS OF MEDITATION

Reviewing 112 different meditative techniques, Osho (1974) discovered commonalities and posited three fundamentals, regardless of the specific method used. These principles could help you in your own practice and when facilitating in the classroom.

Relax

While traditions such as Zen Buddhism place much emphasis on how to sit, meditation, as it's being presented in this book for the college classroom, doesn't require any particular posture. Chapter 5 addresses guidance on meditating while in a chair (which is likely how students will meditate). The bottom line is to be comfortable—relaxed but alert.

Witnessing

Once in a comfortable position, begin watching or witnessing. What you witness is not as important as the quality of awareness you are practicing. This means you can watch your breath (as will be discussed in detail later), watch the body and its sensations, watch thoughts, or even listen to sounds. Remember, regardless of the actual technique used, meditation is the process of observing what is happening.

Non-Evaluation

When witnessing, do not evaluate what is happening or what you are observing. For instance, when thoughts arise in the mind or memories surface, simply watch without judging them. Judging the experience will counteract the meditative state, which is one of open acceptance. While judgment and analyzation are deeply ingrained in our psyche, these mental processes directly counter meditation. Lizzie (2017) skillfully articulates this:

> The mind will want to judge it, to analyze it and to give it a pat on the back, or to admonish it. But to judge meditation misses the point of it. The real purpose of meditation is to understand the nature of the mind. It is not about emptying the mind, but looking into it. It is about deepening your awareness of what is there, understanding it and exploring it (n.p.).

COMMON MISCONCEPTIONS ABOUT MEDITATION

There exist misconceptions and misinformation regarding meditation, which can make it difficult for students (or anyone) to learn. Like the above essentials, this information has been woven into the meditation facilitation guide found in Chapter 9. Having a clear understanding of these misconceptions and how to address them is critical to facilitation.

No Thoughts Allowed

Somewhere along the way, meditation was presented as a mental activity that involved completely clearing the mind of thoughts—complete clarity. Meditation is not the same as concentration. Concentration requires a narrowing of consciousness through the elimination of stimuli; meditation is the opposite. It is inclusiveness, becoming aware of whatever enters one's consciousness.

While meditation, over time, can reduce the train of thoughts, the idea that one cannot meditate if they have thoughts is a wrong notion that will prevent someone from properly learning. Thoughts are completely natural, and during meditation, it is completely normal to have thoughts, sometimes *lots of thoughts*. Also, meditation didn't create the frenzy of thoughts you may experience; rather, sitting in meditation allowed you to become aware of what was already happening in your mind, like turning on the lights in a dark house and suddenly noticing the furniture, the dust, and the cobwebs in the corner.

Meditation is not about controlling thoughts or stopping them but experiencing them in a nonjudgmental manner, allowing them to come and go like clouds passing in the sky or traffic down a street. This witnessing of thoughts is the appropriate way to address them since thinking, like your heartbeat, is natural and goes on automatically.

Stop reading for a minute and try this short experiment. Sit with your eyes closed and begin to notice your thoughts. Now, stop your thoughts—all of them. After completely turning them off, how did it go? What happened? Trying to stop your thinking likely increased your thinking. Fighting against thoughts creates even more mental activity. So it's critical to understand this concept and explain it to students. Allow thoughts to come and go, watch them, observe them, appreciate them—but do not evaluate them or work against them. The mere witnessing of thoughts, in time, will allow them to diminish. The mind will find its own clarity in its own time. Just patience is needed.

Meditation Is a Mysterious, Esoteric Practice

There is nothing mysterious about meditation (at least these days). Meditation involves tapping into innate human capabilities (awareness, alertness, etc.) that we already possess. It's more the experience of remembering or rediscovering. As Tibetan Buddhist monk Ricard (2015) said, "There's nothing mysterious. You don't need to be sitting trying to empty your mind with incense around you under the mango tree."

Meditation Is Serious Business and Hard Work

Yes, meditation requires an investment of time and patience. However, the proper attitude toward meditation is one of play, relaxation, and enjoyment. Going into meditation with an attitude of strain and effort counteracts the requirement that one is relaxed to enter a meditative state. "Playing" with the idea of meditation and bringing a sense of enjoyment to it allows meditation to naturally do its work. Meditation is a spontaneous process. It happens on its own accord. What you must do is set up the proper conditions for this to occur. In addition, meditation for its own sake—relaxing at your center, giving the mind a rest—is its own benefit.

Meditation Takes a Lot of Time

Meditation teachers may recommend that practitioners meditate for 30–60 minutes per day. Some traditions, such as Transcendental Meditation, suggest sitting for two periods per day, once in the morning and once in the later afternoon. While meditating for longer sessions may produce more benefits, even a few minutes of meditation can help produce some calm and a sense of ease. College students have reported that just sitting quietly in the classroom for a few minutes listening to the sound of a bell or witnessing their breath can reduce tension (Haberlin, 2021). One study of 181 psychology and kinesiology college students found that just by having them listen to a three-minute mindfulness meditation or sit silently during class, twice per week, produced improvements in patience and emotional valence, increased awareness, and decreased reactivity to inner experience (Kirby et al., 2021).

Meditation Is a Religious (Non-Secular) Practice

While meditation techniques and methods are grounded in various traditions such as Buddhism, meditation itself does not belong to a particular culture or religion. The practice of sitting quietly, observing one's breath or thoughts, and being present in the moment is a natural state that can be enjoyed by everyone. The practice of meditation does not require belief in a particular god or higher power—or any belief at all. It simply involves understanding the meditative process and being familiar with the working of the mind and consciousness.

There Is Only One Way to Meditate

While the word "meditation" may conjure up thoughts of a person sitting crossed-legged, perfectly still, on a tropical beach somewhere, a variety of ways of meditating exist, and they don't all include assuming a certain posture or even being still. Meditation is a state of pure awareness, and how that is experienced by the individual differs. Some may reach this state sitting on the floor, observing their breath, or repeating a mantra, while for others, meditation is arrived at through walking, yoga, or even running. In Chapter 4, you will learn more about specific methods when designing a personal practice.

Meditation Is Only about Reducing Stress

Although helping students de-stress through brief meditation may be the focus of this book, meditation expands beyond this goal. Traditionally, for example, within Buddhism, meditation has been a vehicle for exploring meaning and purpose in life, for developing compassion and positive states of mind and seeking enlightenment. Meditation as stress reduction has been embraced by Westerners, which is perfectly fine, though we should remember this is only a "side effect" of practice and not the only reason to meditate.

Meditation Is Only a Solitary Practice

While meditation is about learning to enjoy one's own company, and you may spend much time meditating by yourself, meditation can also be experienced in the presence of others (as in the case of inviting students to meditate in your classroom). Meditating in a group setting can lend a powerful boost to one's practice. As meditation teacher Susan Shumsky (2001) explains, when people meditate together, the experiences of relaxation, peace of mind, and expanded awareness are intensified.

WHAT'S NEXT?

With a solid conceptual understanding of meditation, we will get into specific meditation methods and techniques that can be effectively embedded into the college classroom. These techniques do not take a long time to learn, nor do they require long periods of practice, making them ideal to use before academic instruction.

CHAPTER SUMMARY

- Meditation is a state of non-doing. It is an intrinsic state of pure awareness with no content.
- The practice of meditation dates back thousands of years and can be found in various traditions around the world, including Buddhism, Hinduism, and Christianity.
- Meditation works by allowing you to become more familiar with the inner workings of your mind and consciousness.
- The fundamentals of meditation are being in a relaxed position, witnessing or observing, and non-evaluation of the experience. The idea that meditation is exhausting, concentrative mental work that involves completely blanking out the mind is a misconception.

Chapter 4

Developing Your Meditation Practice (as a Stressed-Out Academic?)

The focus of this book is incorporating meditation into to your classroom as a way to assist students with stress, anxiety, and distractions. But what about you? What are you doing to manage stress, to center, to increase clarity and well-being? How are you maintaining the mental and emotional fuel needed to lead students? This chapter is geared toward understanding how to develop and maintain your own meditation practice. Think of it as a much-needed sidebar. Engaging in a personal contemplative practice will not only provide personal benefit but aid you in facilitating meditation with students at a deeper level, one coming from your authenticity and experience.

THE STRESSED-OUT PROFESSOR

Working as an academic has become increasingly challenging and stressful. Depending on what college or university you work at, you must juggle many responsibilities, from teaching heavy course loads to serving on committees, completing administrative studies, advising students, and feeling pressure to conduct research and publish papers. Despite this complexity, teaching in itself can "generate a high level of anxiety, depression, stress, and fatigue" (Ferreira-Vorkapic et al., 2018, p. 216). Teaching in academia can involve long hours planning classes and being in the classroom, large class sizes, dealing with difficult students, and having to adapt to new curricula and teaching approaches such as the use of technology. As you read this, these stressors likely resonate—and you likely can think of others.

The COVID-19 pandemic, however, pushed the stress of higher education faculty to peak levels. According to a study by Course Hero (2020) of more than 570 full- and part-time faculty, more than half reported experiencing symptoms related to workplace burnout. Nearly 75 percent of faculty attributed their main source of stress to having to transition to new modes of teaching (for example, hybrid and online learning). About two-thirds of the study reported significant stress from trying to meet the mental and emotional needs—what's known as the impact of secondary trauma—of students. Faculty involved with the study advocated for increased pay, lighter course loads, and more assistance. While these factors can certainly help with job satisfaction and stress, they are not entirely in your control. What can you do? How might you deal with increased stress on the job in healthy ways?

THE CONTEMPLATIVE ACADEMIC

Well, you probably guessed that you can meditate. While there is little research at the moment focusing specifically on meditation and higher education faculty and their stress, one study's findings echo benefits being experienced by general populations of adults. In the study (Ferreira-Vorkapic et al., 2018), 60 college professors (men and women between the ages of 30 and 55 years old) were randomly placed in one of three experimental groups. Two groups were instructed in either seated meditation or *Yoga Nidra,* which involves lying down and engaging in guided relaxation meditation. College professors practicing the meditative interventions showed significant decreases in stress and anxiety as compared with the control group.

Since burnout results from chronic work-related stress, meditation has been recommended for workers in general as a possible intervention. Mindfulness meditation, for instance, has been found to improve physiological indicators of stress, such as decreased cortisol (Gabriel & Aguinis, 2022; Heckenberg et al., 2018). However, stress reduction is not the only reason to meditate as an academic.

IS YOUR CUP FULL?

There is a popular story about a professor who visits a Zen master. Upon meeting the master, the professor launches into a discourse about how much he has read on the subject of Zen and how much he has learned. During this time, the Zen master, who is pouring the professor a cup of tea, continues pouring though the cup is overflowing. The professor blurts out, "Stop! Why are you still pouring? The cup is full!" To which the master calmly replies, "Like this cup, your mind is already full. Unless you empty it, there is nothing I can teach you."

Along with stress reduction, meditation is being explored in academia as a vehicle to promote openness and a greater sense of awareness (known in Zen as "beginner's mind"). "Professors would benefit from developing a greater sense of wakefulness or being in the moment, to welcome diverse perspectives that might aid these new ways of doing and being" (Brendel & Cornett-Murtada, 2019, p. 5). Let's face it: as academics, we often get stuck in our heads, we intellectualize. This is par for the course of the job. However, without an expanded sense of awareness that meditation brings, this can be limiting. As Brendel & Cornett-Murtada (2019) bravely assert:

> Since university professors are hired to profess, they often succumb to a pride of expertise, marked by endless critique and de facto debate. Over time, this tirelessly analytical habit of mind can become inseparable from professors' personal identities and ways of being. At the same time, many professors genuinely wish to transform student experience and push the boundaries of their own disciplines by practicing greater creativity and self-awareness. (pp. 5–6).

PRACTICING WHAT YOU FACILITATE

There is an anecdote about Mahatma Gandhi, the lawyer turned activist who used nonviolence to free India from British rule. A mother came to him seeking advice on how to prevent her child from eating so much sugar. The woman did not hear back from Gandhi for six months. When asking him about the delay, Gandhi told her that to speak to her son about cutting out sugar, he had to refrain from eating it—only then could he advise her from a position of confidence and authenticity.

Likewise, before exploring meditation in your classroom, it is highly recommended that you first become a meditator. As Barbezat and Bush (2013) explain, "there is no effective way to teach contemplative practices without practicing them yourself. You need a deep familiarity with the practices before introducing them so you can guide students through them" (pp. 67–68).

As meditation teacher Kevin Ellerton (2021) writes, you must have a "deep, subjective knowledge of meditation" (n.p.) in order to guide students and answer their questions. You need to know how it feels to meditate and how it impacts your mind, body, and heart. This can only come through personal experience. Unlike developing content mastery as an academic, where you might read, study, and research information from an intellectual standpoint, meditation involves sustained, first-person inquiry to fully comprehend it. It is a state that must be experienced.

DEVELOPING A PERSONAL MEDITATION PRACTICE

Hopefully, at this point you are convinced of the benefits of establishing your own meditation practice as a precursor to introducing meditation to students. Establishing a personalized meditation practice involves some experimentation. There is no one-size-fits-all approach, as individuals have different needs, dispositions, temperaments, and lifestyles. One of the challenges is that there are a variety of meditation techniques and methods from different traditions—knowing which one is right for you is a matter of trying them out. Other considerations are how often to meditate, where to meditate, and how to know if it's working. The following sections will offer guidance.

Choosing a Meditation Method

Depending on the source, there are at least a half dozen commonly practiced meditation methods. This is by no means an exhaustive list. For instance, *The Book of Secrets* (Osho, 1974) describes 112 variations of meditation techniques. While there is not enough space in this book to provide a comprehensive description of each technique, below are brief descriptions of some common methods.

Mindfulness Meditation

Based on Buddhist teachings, mindfulness meditation involves simply sitting or being in a comfortable position and bringing awareness to your inner state. Without judgment, you observe your thoughts and feelings as they pass. You notice the sensations in your body. You can also gently become aware of the flow of the breath. Possible benefits of this method include increased self-awareness, decreased stress levels and response, more awareness of thoughts and emotions, and the refocusing of attention.

Vipassana *(Breath Meditation)*

This technique requires paying attention to the natural rhythm of the breath. There is a detailed description for *vipassana* in Chapter 5.

Mantra Meditation

During this meditation, the practitioner uses a mantra, or sound, which is gently repeated in the mind. When you have thoughts or become distracted, you simply return your attention to repeating the mantra. Possible benefits include retraining the wandering mind, improved physical and mental well-being, and reduced stress and anxiety. Transcendental Meditation is a form of mantra meditation. More information is available at www.tm.org.

Heart Meditation

These practices involve generating positive emotions, such as love and compassion. Loving-Kindness is a popular method in this category (this technique is mentioned in more depth in Chapter 7, as a possible extension for students). Possible benefits from this method include enhanced relationships, improved emotional well-being, and increased feelings of self-love. For guidance in these practices, you might refer to the work of Sharon Salzberg (sharonsalzberg.com) and Jack Kornfield (jackkornfield.com).

Moving Meditation

If you struggle with sitting quietly, moving meditation such as Tai Chi, Qigong, yoga, or walking meditation might resonate. These movement-based methods require bringing awareness to motion and can help improve health, reduce stress, and improve overall clarity of the mind and well-being. Running can also be a powerful vehicle for meditation, as one is immersed in natural surroundings, moving freely, and falling in rhythm with the breath. Similarly, surfing can provide the perfect grounds for tuning into a meditative state.

MEDITATION SELF-ASSESSMENT

The Chopra Center (Williams, 2018) recommends completing a self-assessment before selecting a meditation method. Consider the following questions as you research a technique that best fits:

- What do you feel is lacking in your life?
- How does your body feel? Are there any places where it feels heavy or stuck?
- Do you have a lot on your mind (more than usual)?
- Do you need help focusing?
- How do you want to feel (nourished, connected, energized, purposeful, etc.)?

In addition, consider the following factors when exploring the ideal meditation method: time, energy level, and motivation (Osho Sammasati, n.d.). Given your current schedule, how much time can you dedicate to meditation practice—10 minutes, 30 minutes, or 60 minutes per day? Some methods require more time than others. Also consider your present energy level and mobility. Are you seeking a more active technique or something that provides more rest and recharging? Finally, what is your motivation? Are you needing a tool to de-stress, raise energy, navigate emotions, or improve relationships?

Reflect on the following kinds of questions within the context of your work as an academic:

- What method might best complement your current teaching and scholarship?
- What challenges (stress, creativity, mental clarity) are present in your work?
- What methods might your students benefit from and/or be practicing? How might that help you implement these methods in your classroom?

What Clicks?

A more direct approach to selecting a meditation method is to pick a method, try it for a week, and see if it "clicks." See if the method resonates or brings a sense of enjoyment. If so, commit to it for several months, practicing once or twice a day, if possible (Osho, 1974). Since meditation is all about direct experience and self-inquiry, just diving right in will provide you with the experience to judge whether a method is right for you. After trying a method, if it doesn't feel right or comfortable, choose another method and try that one. Additionally, a particular meditation method might work for you, but over time, it becomes routine and needs to be dropped. For example, I practiced mantra meditation for years, experiencing benefits, but felt the need to experiment with other methods as time passed.

How Long Should You Meditate?

After choosing a method, a common question is "How long should I meditate?" Again, answers vary, but generally, meditation experts recommend starting gradually and building up the time you meditate each session. Similarly, when starting a new workout, it's not advisable to spend two hours at the gym—endurance must be built up over time.

With meditation, start in small increments, like five to 10 minutes, and increase over time. Ideally, you might spend 20–30 minutes in the morning in meditation and possibly meditate again in the evening. You can really meditate at any time of the day, but establishing a practice in the morning sets the tone for the day and allows for meditation to happen before you get busy with your day. If possible, you can engage in a second session in the evening, perhaps before dinner or after a long day of work to help unwind and throw off stress.

However, while quantity and frequency are often mentioned, the quality of meditation is what matters most (Osho, 1969). Discovering a meditation technique that personally enables you to experience deeper meditation states is key; otherwise, sitting for hours will not spark any transformation.

Where to Meditate?

While you can meditate anywhere, try to designate a specific place, such as a bedroom, a corner of the room, or an outdoor patio, as your regular meditation spot. Meditating in the same place every day creates a supportive energy and lets the mind know it's time to remain quiet and engage in non-doing. You can have a comfortable chair or floor mats in the space. Hang inspiring pictures, bring fresh flowers to the spot, and light incense if that incites relaxation and calm. However, depending on your schedule, this might not always be practical. Luckily, meditation is mobile and, if necessary, can be practiced wherever you are. As meditation teacher Dan Harris explains, "I meditate in the back of taxicabs, in airplanes, in my bedroom while the kid is freaking out, in my office" (Graves, 2022, n.p.). Meditating around natural elements, such as a wooded area, a park, or a stream, can support your practice.

When to Meditate?

Essentially, you can meditate anytime you find time. It's often suggested that you meditate upon waking up in the morning, before breakfast, to set the tone for the day and before you get too busy with life's responsibilities. If possible, engaging in a second meditation in the early evening, after the workday but before dinner, can help you de-stress from the day. Experiment with different times to determine what works best. Here are some other suggestions:

- Meditate when you feel you're getting stressed out or overwhelmed. This can take the edge off. Often, when we think we are too busy to meditate is when meditation is most needed.
- During your lunch break, meditate as a way to de-stress, recharge, and gain clarity.
- Before bedtime, meditate as a way to prepare for a deeper sleep. A brief meditation, perhaps an hour or two before sleeping, might settle the mind and body. However, meditating too close to shut-eye could keep some people up as it brings a boost of energy.
- Meditate while in the shower or bath. The warm, flowing water could help the meditation process.

- Finally, avoid meditating on a full stomach. Give yourself at least an hour or two to eat before meditation practice. Eating prior to meditation activates the digestive system and makes the body more active, countering the process of meditation, which slows metabolism.

Sustaining Your Meditation Practice

More important than how long you meditate is that you meditate every day and you are consistent. Thus, getting back to the question of time, set a manageable amount of time and build up from there. To make your practice sustainable, try linking it to other habits, such as rising and having a cup of coffee or brushing your teeth. Right after, say, brushing your teeth, you sit and meditate.

Another key is to just show up physically, or as Sharon Salzberg (2011) teaches, "put your body there" (n.p.). She also advises that if your resolve for meditation practice weakens, it's natural to just begin again. Perhaps read some inspiring poetry or join a group of meditators to help find inspiration. Guided meditations can be an effective way to not only learn a method but assist in sticking with it. Another strategy to maintain your practice is to keep a meditation journal. Furthermore, if you miss a meditation or stop practicing, you can always begin again.

A NOTE ON MEDITATION APPS

While there's no replacement for learning meditation from a teacher, technology has birthed a myriad of meditation apps. Accessing these apps could be a way to get started through guided meditations. While some studies suggest that meditation apps can lower stress and increase general well-being (Bostock et al., 2019), there's a lack of research to confirm whether apps produce a significant effect (Gál et al., 2021). One limitation reported among popular meditation apps is that, while they guide one through the process, they provide "limited support for monitoring the intrinsic meditation processes or for measuring the effectiveness of the training" (Daudén & Sas, 2018, p. 5). Below is a list of paid and free apps.

Calm

This meditation app comes highly recommended, as it provides a host of short, guided meditations. Calm offers a seven-day trial, and an annual subscription runs about $70.

Insight Timer

This app provides some free resources, including access to various guided meditations. It also features virtual singing bowls and bell sounds you can use in the classroom or for personal practice. A premium membership costs about $60 a year.

Headspace

This is another popular app with hundreds of guided meditations for all levels. An annual subscription costs about $70.

Smiling Mind

This not-for-profit app is completely free and offers a host of guided meditation resources, including those for use in the classroom.

Live Awake Podcast

This resource, hosted by Sarah Blondin, provides free guided meditation.

HOW DO I KNOW IT'S WORKING?

While it's not advisable to continuously evaluate your meditation, your mind will naturally want to know, *Is this working?* Meditation can take time to produce results; however, one should be careful not to judge it based entirely on individual settings. Some meditation sessions will feel pleasant, even blissful; however, others might feel uncomfortable or emotionally challenging. As Salzberg (2011) writes, "meditation is never one thing; you'll experience moments of peace, moments of sadness, moments of joy, moments of anger, moments of sleepiness. The terrain changes constantly, but we tend to solidify it around the negative" (n.p.).

Rather than judge your practice based on experiences during meditation, look to your daily life as the test. While it's difficult to pinpoint specific benefits since meditation is highly personalized, here are some possible checkpoints:

- Do you feel calmer in situations that would normally trigger you or make you anxious or stressed?
- Do you feel more relaxed or more energetic?

- Are you getting more done in the same amount of time and with less stress?
- Do your relationships seem smoother?
- Are you more present-centered (less worrying about the future and less living in the past)?
- Do you have a greater appreciation and more enjoyment for the small joys of life?

Meditation Journal

You may want to keep a meditation journal to track your progress and experiences. Yoga teacher Michelle Dalbec (n.d.) believes that meditation and journaling are complementary, as they both are tools to explore our interiority. She teaches:

> When we put thoughts to paper—or type them—we are able to clear our mind and gain perspective on any given situation. Journaling gives our internal landscape a voice. It's a chance to document our process, to reflect upon and release our longings and questions. By combining meditation and journaling, you can access the wisdom from the deeper layers of your being and develop a greater understanding of the messages they have to offer. (n.p.)

Dalbec recommends spending about five minutes each day journaling after meditation. Journal from "a place of spaciousness," allowing your writing to be organic and intuitive, perhaps freestyling your words.

Meditation Progress Checklist

To further guide your reflections, the following checklist was comproed from various meditation experts and sources (see Bodhipaksa, 2007; Lennon, 2021; Tadwalkar, n.d.). Remember, meditation is highly individualized, so the results will vary, as well as when and how changes unfold. Thus, the indicators below may or may not apply but can serve as a useful framework for journaling and making sense of your meditation experiences.

MEDITATION PROGRESS CHECKLIST

Indicators:

___ I have noticed improved cognitive functioning (i.e., the ability to concentrate when working/learning, memory seems enhanced, thinking is more fluid, and creative solutions come easier).

___ I fall asleep quicker; my sleep also seems deeper, more refreshing.

___ My physical health seems better (e.g., fewer colds, less-tense and fewer headaches, allergies improved).

___ I feel more comfortable with uncertainty and change.

___ My thoughts (in and out of meditation) seem more present-centered rather than based in the past (memories) or the future (planning).

___ I fall into meditation easier; it seems more natural and comfortable. I rely less on supportive tools, such as obsessing over whether I am focusing on the breath or mantra.

___ My meditation practice has become more of a priority. I find myself practicing consistently.

___ I am judging/evaluating myself less during meditation practice.

___ I find myself slipping into meditation states/moments more throughout the day.

___ Outside of meditation sessions, I notice my breathing more. I may also notice physical sensations in my body that I previously didn't notice.

___ I am more aware of my thoughts and actions. There seems to be more "space" or a gap between when I think and act. I feel like I have more choice in my response to the world around me.

___ I am more aware of my emotions, including when I begin to get angry.

___ I am enjoying simple pleasures more and feeling more connected to the environment. For example, I enjoy walking more, my morning cup of coffee, seeing the sunset or sunrise, or hearing the birds chirping.

___ Others are noticing that I have changed (e.g., more relaxed, less reactive).

___ I am not annoyed or annoyed as often by things that normally bothered me (e.g., traffic jams, waiting in lines, comments by others).

___ I have stopped comparing my meditations (this was a "good" meditation, this was a "bad" one).

WHAT'S NEXT?

Ideally, this chapter has motivated you to begin a meditation practice. Experiment with methods and take a course with a meditation teacher if possible. If not, try a guided meditation using an app or follow instructions laid out in Chapter 7. With firsthand experience, the next step is to introduce meditation into your classroom.

CHAPTER SUMMARY

- Working in academia has been more challenging and stressful due to added responsibilities, more difficult students, and having to learn new modes of teaching, including virtual instruction.
- Developing a personal meditation practice can help reduce stress but also better prepare faculty to facilitate meditation techniques in the classroom.
- Choosing a meditation technique that is the right fit requires some reflection experimentation.
- Create a sustainable practice by gradually increasing time spent in meditation and noticing the results that show up in daily life.

Chapter 5

Vipassana and Other Meditation Methods for the College Classroom

HOW DO STUDENTS ACTUALLY MEDITATE?

Hopefully, after establishing your own meditation practice, a major part of facilitating meditation in your classroom is knowing how to instruct students in some basic meditation techniques. Meditation is a state of non-doing where one is relaxed, centered, and experiencing awareness with no attachment to mental content. However, to reach that state, various techniques and methods have been developed. The aim of this chapter is not to present a comprehensive list of these methods, but rather to provide a detailed explanation of a few methods that have worked well in the college classroom.

As explained earlier, meditation techniques are generally lumped into two types: (1) those that are more concentrative in nature, and (2) those that involve experiencing more open awareness. For example, meditation traditions such as Buddhism have used the breath as an object of attention, a reference point, when the mind naturally wanders. Another device used as a support during meditation is a mantra, a sound that is gently repeated mentally.

Why are meditative techniques needed in the first place if meditation is our natural state? Well, in Zen Buddhism, for instance, practitioners meditate at times by simply "sitting." Facing a wall, they may sit for 40 minutes, an hour, or more, doing nothing. Meditation being a highly individualized experience, this simply does not work for everyone. Try an experiment: Sit for several minutes, doing absolutely nothing—not using a meditation technique—and see what happens. The conditioned mind will often fiercely resist this experience, feeling almost impossible to some. Thus, methods are needed to calm the mind, gently direct the mind, and eventually surpass the thinking mind to a state of meditation.

To implement meditation in the college classroom, what's needed are methods that do not require substantial amounts of time to learn or difficult postures that can't be accomplished sitting at a classroom desk, but ones that produce an immediate (or fairly immediate) sense of calm and focus. Thus, methods such as *vipassana*, or breath meditation, and mindfulness meditations, such as the body scan and listening mindfully, are ideal (this is based on actual experience in the college classroom).

INTENTIONS OF CLASSROOM MEDITATION

Before proceeding to specific meditation techniques to introduce to students, it's necessary to outline some of the goals set forth within this book regarding the hopeful outcomes of meditation in the college classroom. Realistically, students will not reach spiritual enlightenment, major inner transformation, or higher levels of consciousness by participating in brief meditation sessions prior to instruction—nor should this be the goal. Moreover, students will not become experienced meditators or meditation experts through your facilitation. These ideals were never the intent of the original Micro-Meditation project. Rather, the following were the realistic, healthy intentions of the project:

1. Help students de-stress and focus prior to starting classes.
2. Share simple meditation techniques to calm the mind and relax the body (that could also be practiced independently outside of the classroom if that was the desire).
3. Create a classroom ritual or tradition that appreciates pausing and taking a moment for oneself and to connect with others.
4. Explore meditation as another pedagogical tool to foster a supportive, inclusive, enriching learning community.

Keeping these intentions in mind will support your work in embedding brief meditation into the culture of the classroom and allow you to better gauge results.

THE "REQUIRED INSTRUCTION" DILEMMA

It also should be noted that meditation experts often encourage beginners to complete in-person instruction at workshops or retreats. S. N. Goenka, who reintroduced *vipassana* to India and later the world, and the Vipassana

Research Institute recommend that the method be learned during a 10-day retreat. Other methods, like Transcendental Meditation, require learning the technique during four consecutive days of personal instruction. Hence, the dilemma: Should college faculty go ahead and introduce meditation techniques, forgoing these suggestions?

Perhaps professors can dedicate time to personally learning meditation methods (during a winter or summer break or sabbatical), but expecting large numbers of students to personally complete these types of instruction is highly impractical.

A TASTE OF MEDITATION

One way to view the situation is that introducing students to meditation, even briefly, provides them with a glimpse or taste of meditation. As Glickman (2002) writes, if some instruction isn't provided and people can only learn through intensive, in-person retreats, as in the case of *vipassana*, "they will never end up trying it, never getting a visceral sense of how it works and feels" (p. 9). By exposing students to meditation, several outcomes can happen. They don't enjoy it or experience benefits and thus opt out during class time (to be discussed later); they experience some stress relief, calm, and clarity before class; or, in a best-case scenario, they pursue additional meditation instruction or establish their own practice.

Faculty aspiring to introduce students to meditation should be inspired by studies, such as one by Tang and colleagues (2007) in which just five days of meditation practice resulted in significantly better attention and control of stress than for students who did not practice. Students involved in the study learned a Chinese technique called Integrative Body-Mind Training, which uses guided instruction to help practitioners achieve a state of restful awareness. The students learned the technique on the first day and practiced as a group for the remaining days. Thus, if the goal is to help our students relax and focus, lengthy, intensive meditation training is unnecessary.

A FEW WORDS ON POSTURE

When introducing various meditation methods, it's necessary to address how students should sit, or posture. Traditions such as Zen Buddhism place great emphasis on posture during meditation. Everything from how straight the spine should be, how the head and chin are held at a certain angle, how the hips align with the shoulders, to how the hands are placed is addressed. Engaging in classroom meditation presents a unique situation since most likely students will be sitting in chairs at tables or desks. Unless you have nontraditional seating in your classroom, such as cushions or mats, it's not relevant to discuss meditating in a traditional, cross-legged position on the floor, for instance. What follows, then, is a list of tips for guiding students who will be meditating in classroom chairs.

- Advise the students that sitting with the back straight (but not stiff) can help promote a state of alertness. They can imagine their spine is like a stack of coins, going straight up. Another image could be that of a string tied to the top of the head, extending toward the ceiling. Scooting to the edge of the chair may help.
- Keep the feet flat on the floor, creating a 90-degree angle with the knees. Having the feet firmly planted creates a sense of groundedness.
- Instruct the students to easily rest the hands on the lap or knees. Palms can be facing upward. The important thing is not to be tense (for example, having the hands balled up into fists).
- The chin can be tucked slightly down.
- Eyes can be closed or easily gazing downward.
- The students could be encouraged to bring in their own pillows, which could be placed under the seat of the chair as a cushion or placed against the back of the chair (near the lower back) for support.
- Finally, tell the students to experiment with posture. As Josa (2012) notes, "it can feel strange meditating on a chair. But that's ok. Just go with it for a week or so. Tweak your posture until you feel upright and comfortable" (n.p.).

VIPASSANA **IN THE CLASSROOM**

Vipassana, sometimes called breath meditation or mindfulness meditation, is a technique of observing the breath. The Pali word *vipassana* is often translated as *insight* or seeing. *Vipassana* meditation was rediscovered by the Buddha 2,600 years ago and served as the essence of his meditation practices. *Vipassana* is described as a simple, practical, secular technique that can produce feelings of calm and peace of mind (Vipassana Research Institute, n.d.), making it suitable for helping students in your classroom settle their minds, de-stress, and focus on learning new content. Furthermore, the technique does not require any special postures or clothing and can be practiced anywhere. "With Vipassana, it's really a case of come as you are, bring with you all of your life's content, and release it to breathe your way to change" (Silva, 2020, p. 4).

What makes *vipassana* so effective is that it draws from both single-pointed, concentrative-type techniques, by using the breath as a support or frame of reference, and more open-awareness-based methods, by being sensitive to sensations and experiences that arise. As Glickman (2002) explains, "it combines the best elements of both methods" (p. 40). Interestingly, there is a direct correlation between the breath and thoughts. As the breath naturally slows and deepens when observed over time, thoughts also decrease. Think of the breath when you are angry or excited, how it operates quickly and in a shallow manner, and how thoughts during these emotional states correspond. Well, the opposite holds true. As we relax and the breath slows, the mind also slows and gains clarity.

How to Practice *Vipassana*

While there are various approaches to teaching *vipassana*, this version is based on Glickman's (2002) instructions, which are based on the teachings of S. N. Goenka. These instructions and guidelines have been infused into the meditation facilitation guide for the classroom detailed in Chapter 9, thus faculty can see how to weave in these instructions and what language to use with students.

Working with the Breath (*Anapana*)

Begin by sitting comfortably. It's not necessary to sit on the floor with legs crossed. Sitting in a chair is perfectly fine (which is what students will likely be doing in your classroom). The position should be "upright and comfortable" and one should feel "relaxed yet alert" (Glickman, 2002, p. 81). The chin can be slightly pointed down. The eyes can be closed or slightly closed, gazing softly at an imaginary point three or four feet away on the ground (encourage students to find what works best for them; note that some may not be comfortable closing their eyes completely). The hands should be relaxed on the legs, with palms facing up or cupped.

Now, gently turn the attention to the breath. "Breathing naturally, observe the sensations the touch of the breath makes in the area of the nostrils" (Glickman, 2002, p. 87). When your attention wanders and you have thoughts (which is inevitably going to happen), gently return your awareness to the natural flow of the breath. Remember, as explained in Chapter 3, do not fight thoughts when they occur—simply observe them without judgment. Watch them come and go. You may also experience feelings and emotions arising. Allow them space to emerge but remain objective and nonjudgmental. The same goes for any distractions, such as hearing outside noises (passing traffic, barking dog). Just observe the phenomena and easily return your attention to the breath.

If it helps, you can experiment with focusing the attention on the temperature of the breath as it enters the nostrils (cool) and leaves (warm). You can pay attention to the area below the nostrils and above the upper lip. You can also focus on the navel—how the belly rises and falls with each breath. What's important isn't what you watch, but the quality of awareness and attitude of openness and nonjudgment.

You may notice the breath begins to deepen and/or slow down. The body may start to feel more relaxed. The mind may have fewer thoughts and feel more open and expansive; however, especially when first practicing meditation, the mind can appear busier. Meditation is a personal, individualized practice, so experiences will differ. Whatever happens, simply witness it.

Sometimes, even after just a few minutes, students practicing *vipassana* in the classroom will report feeling a sense of calm. Their scattered, anxious minds settle, and they feel more open and ready to engage with others and new academic content. One student explained her experience this way (Haberlin, 2021):

> While I was doing this every week in class, it allowed for me to have a moment of calmness and peace for that minute. I allowed myself to feel what my body was telling me and think about nothing. There were some moments when I thought to myself, "Can my life get any crazier?" and then I would snap out of it and just kick out the negative thoughts in my head.

Another student had this experience with *vipassana*:

> I think it helps me to focus more. When I'm coming in from outside, getting up in the mornings, my brain is kind of like everywhere, thinking about everything, and it brings me back to what am I doing, right? Okay, let's focus, and throughout the class period, I can focus more on what you are saying, connect more to the material. I am more open to learning, more motivated to listen to what you are saying.

The Body Scan

Another mindfulness meditation that can be done in the classroom is the mindfulness body scan. Although typically done lying down, the body scan technique can be practiced sitting in a chair. The method is straightforward and doesn't take a long time to learn, making it practical for the classroom. Again, there are variations of this method, but the body scan generally involves systematically sensing through the body with one's mind, bringing awareness to various regions (Kabat-Zinn, 2005). Practicing the body scan enables the meditator to become more in tune and familiar with bodily sensations, both pleasant and unpleasant. Becoming more sensitive to the body's sensations and energy, one also becomes more attuned to how they hold and experience stress in the body and how the body reacts or responds to experiences and situations. College students often find that even a brief body scan can help them locate their stress, become more aware of it, and begin to release and relax it.

Begin the body scan method by bringing gentle awareness to the top of the head, sensing into the area, just observing the sensations that already exist. As with *vipassana*, there is no judgment, but simple, open awareness of what is happening. Slowly move your attention down to the forehead, feeling or sensing into the region. Continue moving the attention down, through the eyes, nose, and mouth, and to the jaw, allowing it to relax.

If you notice tension in a particular area, don't try to relax—just keep the awareness there, and if it helps, observe the breath as well. Bring the attention down into the shoulders, allowing them to drop if that feels comfortable. Allow the attention to scan down the arms through the triceps, biceps, and forearms, settling into the hands, sensing into the muscle tissue. Feel the energy that circulates through the fingers.

Then, scan back up through the arms to the chest area, feeling any sensations in the heart area. Move down the sternum to the abdomen, allowing the stomach muscles to loosen. Bring the awareness to the hips and buttocks, then the thighs, sensing into each area, perhaps feeling a sense of heaviness. Finally, bring the awareness down through the calves, ankles, and into the feet. Allow your mind to work through the soles and the toes, feeling the energy.

After systematically scanning various regions, you can complete the meditation by experiencing the body as a whole, allowing the mind to pick up any sensations (e.g., pain, aches, tingling, tension, relaxation, lightness, heaviness) that arise. When ready, slowly open your eyes.

Abridged Body Scan for the Classroom

The following is a condensed version of the body scan awareness technique, which might be more suitable for classroom use. It focuses on bringing the awareness to four major areas: (1) the neck and shoulders, (2) the palms of the hands, (3) the stomach, and (4) the legs and feet.

Begin by having the students sit in a comfortable posture. Direct them to bring attention easily to the flow of the breath. Then, shift the focus to the neck and shoulder area. Tell the students to allow the awareness to gently rest in that area, noticing any tension (we often hold much tension here). After 30–60 seconds, encourage the students to direct their attention to the palms of the hands, keeping them resting easily on the knees or lower abdomen, if possible with palms up and fingers stretched out. Then, have the students move awareness to the stomach area, feeling any tightness and allowing it to "drop." Finally, have them bring their attention to the legs and feet, including the soles and toes, again sensing any stress in this area. After 30 seconds, ask them to come out of the meditation.

Open-Awareness Meditation

Another meditation method that can be learned and done easily in a college classroom is an open-awareness, mindfulness meditation. However, this may be more difficult for some students, and it is recommended this is shared after practicing *vipassana* and the body scan. During this practice, the meditator is aware of all experiences that arise—the breath, bodily sensations, and thoughts. One simply witnesses or "watches" what occurs, again without judgment or evaluating the experience.

To practice this method, sit comfortably, as instructed with *vipassana*. Closing the eyes, turn the attention inward. Allow the awareness to pick up whatever comes to mind: thoughts racing, the breath as it travels into the nostrils, the tension in the neck area. Simply observe what is happening without resisting the experience. Whatever grabs the attention becomes the reference point. Notice how the body responds as you witness it. Perhaps it begins to relax. Same with the breath. Without strain, just notice how the breath might change, slowing its rhythm. Thoughts might also intensify or slow. Memories might surface. A feeling or emotion might come. Allow everything to come and go. Just watch with curiosity and openness. When ready, slowly open your eyes.

Listening Meditation

A fourth technique that's highly suitable for the college classroom is listening meditation. This method involves closing the eyes and simply and mindfully listening to whatever sounds one hears, whether they are noises in the environment (people talking, birds chirping, the air conditioning unit, cars passing on the road) or internal sounds (stomach growling, the breath). Just listening to can bring a sense of calm and help you feel more centered.

To practice this method, sit comfortably and bring your awareness to your ears. Notice what sounds come. Without straining, easily listen to any sounds, as if you were listening to music you enjoyed. Perhaps begin by listening to sounds close to you, such as your breath. Then, systematically expand your radius, listening to noises in the room and outside. Again, don't judge the sounds or begin pondering on them—just allow them to be. Finally, listen to all sounds, near and far, allowing yourself to fall in tune with them. When ready, slowly open your eyes.

When engaging students in this method, you can experiment with having them listen to the sound of a Tibetan Singing Bowl or a chime. Encourage them to close their eyes and listen deeply to the sound of the bell, how it rises and falls and drops away. Ask them to listen to "what remains" after the bell sound has faded. This in itself can be an effective meditation used to start class.

While not all students will embrace the bell, it can really assist in the listening meditation, as one student remarked:

I started working and doing school full-time; I felt like the world was weighing on my shoulders. Every Monday after I would have been in class all day, [course instructor's] class would calm me down with the bowl. When someone would use the bell in the beginning of class, I would feel my heart rate become normal instead of pumping fast. I would hear ringing in my ear even afterward, to help me remain calm. The bowl helped me through a lot this semester.

Layering Methods

While it's generally discouraged to combine meditation methods, some of these techniques seem complementary in the classroom. For instance, you might ask the students to begin with a very brief body scan, locating any tension in the body. After a quick check-in, they could bring their awareness to the breath for a few minutes. Likewise, the students could start by observing their breath for a few minutes and finish the session by feeling any sensations in the body.

How Long Should Students Meditate?

As you have learned in previous chapters, there is no magic number when asking how long one should practice these different methods. Of course, these methods, when woven into academia, must be condensed considerably to be practiced in the short time we have before beginning class. When developing the meditation facilitation guide, meditation with students generally lasted only a few minutes, never longer than five minutes, sometimes as brief as one minute.

The facilitation guide (Chapter 9) will assist with pacing and determining how long a guided meditation in class should take. The advice is this: Do what you can afford to do, even if it's just a minute of meditation. See what happens. On certain days, perhaps you can extend the meditation another minute or two. Maybe your students appear more stressed during certain times of the semester (midsemester or final exams), and spending more time on the meditation activity makes sense. There is always a balance between taking time to meditate and fitting in all the content we must teach. See meditation as an investment that will pay off later.

As one student explained, just a few minutes can make a major difference.

My overall experience with learning and engaging in meditation in class is that it truly helps. I appreciate doing it because it gives me a moment to truly decompress from everything that I had to take care of before class. It really allows me to focus and put all my focus in class. It calms me down as well.

Barriers to Meditation (Including College Students)

Commonly cited barriers—perceptions that prevent individuals from practicing meditation—often include doubt, restlessness, and questioning the possible benefit or value. People learning to meditate might question whether they have the adequate knowledge and skill. For example, college students completing a semester-long mindfulness course questioned the correctness of their knowledge or technique (Sears et al., 2011).

Another reported barrier of the general population to meditation is coming across unpleasant or painful emotional states. As one experienced meditator notes, "you're coming face to face with your own heart and mind, fear, anger, hatred, confusion, frustration and anxiety, all the difficult emotions. . . . That's the whole point. . . . It was certainly challenging" (Komiya et al., 2000, p. 853).

Other barriers reported by would-be meditators, including college students, include boredom, tiredness, and experiencing physical pain (Lomas et al., 2015). Frequent mind wandering has also been cited as a challenge or barrier (Banerjee et al., 2017). Finally, feeling guilty about taking time out for oneself to meditate seems to be a potential barrier (Cohen-Katz et al., 2005).

College students appear to also have their own unique barriers to learning meditation. In my experience, students may view meditation as esoteric or a strange religious practice or ritual, something that makes them uncomfortable. Others may believe they cannot meditate, having tried before on their own or learning from an Internet source. For other college students, meditation seems extremely unpleasant or the idea of sitting still especially for active individuals, such as student athletes, is painful.

In their research, Bamber and Schneider (2020) list three major barriers to meditation for college studentsn: (1) ambivalence toward meditation, "or an internal struggle raging over the extent to which students should have allowed themselves to go along with the experience, and over its consequences"

(Birnbaum, 2008, p. 844); (2) students did not believe they had time to meditate or that it was not a productive use of time; and (3) some experienced a fear or anxiety toward meditation.

Overcoming Barriers

If you are really interested in pinpointing potential barriers to meditation within a particular group or class of students, you might administer the Determinants of Meditation Practice Inventory (DMPI; Williams et al., 2011). The DMPI, which was developed to assist researchers in expanding possible participants in meditation-related studies, asks the completer to consider 14 different statements dealing with barriers. The following is a revised version of the DMPI (Hunt et al., 2020).

After determining potential perceived barriers, what can faculty do about overcoming the perceptions that prevent students from engaging in meditation? Using the statements from the DMPI, let's briefly discuss action steps for each.

I Prefer to Be Accomplishing Something

This barrier can be brought down by talking to students about how meditation—taking time to calm the mind-body system—is actually an investment that can result in increased energy, clarity, and creativity. Mentioned as a possible motivational angle in the next chapter, meditation can be considered similar to taking time to charge one's cell phone; for it to operate at maximum capacity, it must be plugged in and allowed to "rest."

Meditation Might Be Boring

In the next chapter, you will learn about setting the right stage for meditation—one where the energy and atmosphere are playful and celebratory. Also, adding meditation extension activities (Chapter 9) that add movement can demonstrate that meditation is more than simply sitting still.

It Is a Waste of Time to Sit and Do Nothing

Again, this resistance point can be handled by discussing how meditation can enhance performance, improve energy, enhance memory and cognitive function, and provide other benefits. Faculty can explain that, by spending the first few minutes of class time in meditation, the remainder of the class period will be more fruitful.

DETERMINANTS OF MEDITATION PRACTICE INVENTORY—REVISED (DMPI-R)

Following is a list of statements that some people may agree with and other people may disagree with. There are no right or wrong answers. Please circle the response that best represents your thoughts or opinions.

It will be difficult for me to meditate because . . .

1 = Strongly Disagree
2 = Disagree
3 = Neither Agree Nor Disagree
4 = Agree
5 = Strongly Agree

1. I prefer to be accomplishing something.
2. Meditation might be boring.
3. It is a waste of time to sit and do nothing.
4. I don't believe meditation can help me.
5. I don't know much about meditation.
6. I wouldn't know if I were doing it right.
7. There is no quiet place where I can meditate.
8. There is never a time when I can be alone.
9. I don't have time.
10. I'm concerned meditation will conflict with my religion.
11. I wonder if meditation might harm me.
12. My family would think it was unusual.
13. I am uncomfortable with silence.*
14. I can't stop my thoughts.*

Scoring Instructions

$(1 + 2 + 3 + 4)/4$ = Low Perceived Benefit
$(5 + 6)/2$ = Perceived Inadequate Knowledge
$(7 + 8 + 9)/3$ = Perceived Pragmatic Barriers
$(10 + 11 + 12)/3$ = Perceived Cultural Conflict

*Items 13 and 14 are to be used to prompt clinical discussion and are not used to calculate subscale scores.

I Don't Believe Meditation Can Help Me

To work around this barrier, you might mention how meditation is practiced by various individuals in all walks of life, from sports to business to education to psychology. Also, you could challenge them to view meditation as a first-person experiment by having them give it 30 days and see what happens.

I Don't Know Much about Meditation

This is where you, the facilitator, come in. Armed with knowledge from this book, you can explain in simple, understandable terms the concept of meditation, the necessary background, and some methods, including the mechanics of what happens with the mind when meditating. You can take the mystery and mystique out of it.

I Wouldn't Know If I Were Doing It Right

This barrier again is brought down by an experienced meditator, who can guide the students and discuss various checkpoints and indicators of being on the right track.

There Is No Quiet Place Where I Can Meditate

In the next chapter, you will learn how to create a nurturing environment for learning to meditate. This will include a verbal agreement with the students, including those opting to not meditate, to respect the first few minutes of class as a quiet, reflective time that precludes talking or making other noise.

There Is Never a Time When I Can Be Alone

With group meditation in class, this is not a barrier.

I Don't Have Time

Your students do not need to "find time" since we are investing the first few minutes of class time to engage in meditation. If they want to meditate outside of the classroom on their own, perhaps they can begin with five minutes in the morning upon waking.

I'm Concerned Meditation Will Conflict with My Religion

To overcome this barrier, explain to the students that the manner in which meditation is being practiced in class is secular. While they have roots in Buddhism, the methods simply involve sitting quietly and watching the breath or observing the sensations of the body. If this is still a concern, the students have other options—meditation is voluntary.

I Wonder If Meditation Might Harm Me

Explain that it is rare to have adverse reactions during meditation, and if this occurs, it is typically when people participate in rigorous retreats for long periods of meditation.

My Family Would Think It Was Unusual

Tell the students that meditation practice has become much more mainstream. You can provide articles and information on meditation being used in many secular settings, such as schools, medical centers, and the workplace.

I Am Uncomfortable with Silence

Acknowledge with the students that it can be a bit unsettling to sit in silence. As discussed in Chapter 7, you can tell them you will be using a meditation bell or chime to assist their minds.

I Can't Stop My Thoughts

Explain that it is completely normal to have thoughts during meditation, and that the goal is not to block out or eliminate thoughts but rather become more aware of the thinking process.

In summary, addressing barriers to learning meditation requires disseminating accurate, clear information. Faculty can give practical examples and definitions (as shown in Chapter 3) about meditation practice, demonstrating that it is commonly used in a secular manner by large numbers of people across the world. Sharing research and data around meditation also helps inform students and clear up any misconceptions.

The next step is encouraging students to engage in first-person inquiry of meditation. Allow them to sit so that they can experience calm and less stress in sometimes just a matter of minutes. Careful guidance of practice is also necessary (we will get into this more in the next chapter). Gently facilitate meditation in a way that is inviting, encouraging, and supportive. Finally, exposing students to a variety of meditation can assist them in discovering techniques that work for them as individuals (Chapter 8 dives into this topic). Information and experience can bring down barriers to meditation in the college classroom.

WHAT'S NEXT?

Now that you have some knowledge (and can develop experience) with some meditation techniques for the higher education classroom, we will get into specifics about how to introduce meditation to students and later explore how to sequence facilitation, handle concerns, and expand upon these practices, so the students continue to benefit.

CHAPTER SUMMARY

- While meditation can require intense instruction, introducing students to brief meditations gives them a taste of practice and can help with stress and anxiety.
- Provide the students with guidance on sitting in a chair properly when meditating.
- Mindfulness meditation techniques, including *vipassana* and the body scan, are ideal for classroom meditation.
- Discover what potential barriers students have to learning meditation and address them with clear, accurate information.

Chapter 6

Introducing College Students to Meditation

WHERE TO START?

Determining how to best introduce your students to brief meditation can be overwhelming or, at the least, a bit concerning. Many concerns and questions bubble up, such as: *What do I first say to students? How do I unpack the topic of meditation? How do I encourage them to even give it a try? What if students don't want to participate or like it?*

These concerns will be addressed in this chapter, and options to select from in regard to how to best reveal meditation as a classroom practice will be provided. The bottom line is there is no foolproof way, as classroom dynamics and contexts differ. Only you know what will work best with your students. However, there are some basic entry points—angles of approach—for getting students interested in the practice of meditation and seeing the possible benefits.

FIRST THINGS FIRST: THE IMPORTANCE OF "INVITING" THE STUDENTS

As enthusiastic as we may be about meditation, faculty have to remember that even a brief meditation is (still mainly) outside the norm of traditional academia, and some students may not feel comfortable in participating. Hence, it's wise to preface your introduction of meditation as an "invitation." By *inviting* the students, you are making a polite request for them to engage in meditation. You are opening the door, welcoming them to come in, but you are not shoving them through it. You are okay if they decide to not enter.

So the meditation facilitation guide suggests you use a statement like this: "Before we start the class and engage in learning, I'd like to *invite* everyone to participate in a short meditation." This takes the pressure off the students to feel obligated to try meditation or that they're being forced, as it's being imposed by a professor or course instructor. In fact, during data collection for the Meditation Facilitation project, students specifically noted that facilitators should make it a point to state that the meditation is not mandatory and avoid making them feel pressured. Positioning the meditation as an invitation, a voluntary activity at the start of class, provides options for the students. It gives them a way out without feeling guilty or uncomfortable.

Providing Options for Non-Meditators

After inviting the students to meditate, consider providing other options that they can do during this time whenever meditation is done during the semester. The facilitation guide suggests using a phrase like this:

I want to be clear that meditating in class is completely voluntary, and there's no requirement to practice. Think of this as a quiet reflection time before we start learning new content. So if you choose, you can listen to music quietly, engage in prayer, reflect, sit quietly, or sketch. However, it is important that whatever you choose, we maintain a quiet environment for the next few minutes—please no talking or loud music.

This statement gives the students options but also supports creating a quiet, nurturing environment for meditation to happen (more about this in the next chapter). What other activities can students do if they don't want to meditate? The following is not an exhaustive list and can be extended, but here are some ideas.

Sitting Quietly

Students, like the rest of us, are constantly on the move and constantly having to think in this fast-paced world. Maybe they just want to sit quietly for a few minutes, not necessarily doing *vipassana* or another technique, but simply sitting.

Listening to Music

College students often go everywhere with earbuds and love their music. If you are okay with it, students can listen to music that they enjoy, relaxes them, and helps prepare them for class, with the only caveat being that the music is low enough so as not to disturb others.

Sketching or Doodling

Drawing or sketching can be a stress reliever. Students might like the option of just doodling quietly as others meditate. In Chapter 8, an activity called Zentangle will be covered as a way to vary meditation in class.

Contemplative Crafts

Another idea is to allow students who don't want to engage in formal meditation practice to participate in quiet, repetitive activities, such as knitting or crocheting, which can create calm and relaxation. Knitting, for example, has been shown to reduce stress (Abbott et al. , 2013; Clave-Brule et al., 2009).

Reflection or Prayer

Another option for the students could be taking a few minutes to quietly journal or mentally reflect on their day or week. Depending on their religious/spiritual practice, they could also engage in silent prayer or express gratitude.

DEFINING "MEDITATION" FOR THE STUDENTS

After inviting the students to meditate and providing other options, you want to unpack the concept of meditation; students need to have at least a fundamental sense of what meditation is and what it isn't. The challenge is that you don't have a lot of time to accomplish this task. Thus, giving some basic explanations and definitions of meditation might work best. Using some metaphors and analogies can also help enable students to connect what they already know to the state of meditation.

Drawing on what you learned in Chapter 3, here are some brief explanations of meditation to use during the introduction:

- Meditation is a state of relaxed awareness. The body is resting, like during sleep, but the mind is completely awake and aware.
- Meditation is becoming centered and relaxing into yourself.
- Meditation is a natural state where we are completely focused on the present, relaxed, and alert.
- Meditation is bringing awareness to what is happening, inside and out.
- Meditation is turning 180 degrees inward and exploring our minds.

- Meditation is a state of pure consciousness with no content.
- Meditation is just simply "being." It is non-doing.
- Meditation is when the body, mind, and consciousness function together as one.
- Meditation involves using a specific technique as an anchor to relax the mind and body.

Even using such definitions, students may still be unsure what meditation is. We may get some strange looks; therefore, you may want to draw upon some ready-made metaphors and examples. Here are some you can use.

Meditation as a Natural State (That We May Have Stumbled Upon)

Meditation is intentional in creating a state that human beings likely have experienced at some point in their lives. A meditative moment, where one is relaxed, completely aware and alert, immersed in the present, the mind clear of thoughts of the past and future, might have occurred while staring at a sunset, lying near the ocean, or listening to the crashing waves. Others may have experienced a mediative state while engaged in an art project, falling in love, playing a sport, or traveling to another country.

The Mind Is Like the Sky

In discussing meditation, the meditative mind, or our awareness, has often been compared to the sky: open, expansive, and clear. Behind the passing thoughts and turbulence, the true nature of the mind is vast, undisturbed, and spacious.

The Mind as the Ocean

Similarly, the mind has been compared to the ocean. On the surface, it is rough, turbulent, and wavy (our persistent thoughts and emotions), but underneath, toward the bottom layers, the mind is silent, still, and peaceful. Meditation methods are devices that help us navigate the surface to go to these deeper levels of the mind.

Murky Water Glass

If you allow a glass of dirty stormwater to stand, eventually the dirt will settle to the bottom, allowing the water to be clear. The mind, through meditation, can experience clarity if given time to just be.

Monkey Mind

Buddhist monks have used the metaphor of the mind, with its constant chatter, being like a restless monkey, jumping around and in need of taming. Meditation techniques provide an anchor (a banana, if you will) for the monkey mind, gently taming it.

The Dusty Mirror

In this analogy, the mind is likened to a mirror. Over time it gathers dust and debris. Periodically, the mind (like the mirror) must be cleaned. Meditation is like a mental bath, allowing one to clean the slate.

Recharging the Cell Phone

Comedian Jerry Seinfeld, a long-time practitioner of Transcendental Meditation, says meditation is like having a charger for your cell phone. You can plug in and refresh your mind and body, then you are operating at full capacity.

The Snow Globe

For this analogy, you can even use a physical prop. Shake a snow globe and tell the students that normally our minds are cluttered and scattered, like a snow globe when shaken. But when we meditate, we allow things to settle, and the mind becomes still and clear.

ENTRY POINTS

After inviting the students to meditate and defining meditation, faculty have to do a bit of a sales job. We must answer the question "Why should we meditate before class?" Why should even a few minutes of precious instructional time be devoted to this practice? Again, there is not a one-size-fits-all approach to proclaiming the benefits of meditation or convincing students why they should do it. This will depend on your students—what drives them, what their interests are, and where they are in their lives at this moment.

What follows are various angles or entry points to hook your students. Of course, you can use more than one of these approaches or even combine approaches. For example, you may begin talking to the students about the scientific-based benefits of meditation while focusing on the impact of meditation on stress and learning. You can discuss how meditation might enhance creativity and productivity. If you have student athletes in your class, you may discuss how meditation might help them relax and get into "the zone" when playing. The important thing is to know your audience: who your particular students are, what they connect with, and their current needs, both academic and social-emotional? This is more difficult if you are teaching large, lecture-hall-type classes, but you can still aim for common challenges that students face, such as stress and anxiety.

Stress and Anxiety

Considering the rising stress rates among individuals, including college-age students, discussing meditation within the context of stress reduction seems a safe bet. You might ask your students to rate their current stress level from 1–10, and perhaps have them share some strategies they use to reduce and cope with stress. From there, you can segue into how meditation is an effective stress buster.

You might mention how psychologists have learned that meditation practice impacts brain regions that regulate attention and emotional regulation, and meditators are less likely to react negatively and have stressful and worrying thoughts (American Psychological Association, 2019). For instance, after just eight weeks of mindfulness meditation, individuals with general anxiety disorder experienced reduced anxiety-related symptoms and improved stress reactivity and coping (Hoge et al., 2013).

Focus

Another angle you can take, considering we live in the Age of Distraction, is to discuss how meditation can aid the students in sharpening their focus or ability to keep their mind sustained on tasks, including schoolwork. You might ask them how often they get distracted (for example) during class; be prepared to be surprised. You could even try an activity that I have used, which involves having the students tally every time they reach for their cell phones, or have the intention to do so, or just space out during class-time instruction. This will give them a baseline or idea of just how often they lose focus when it's needed. Mention research that demonstrating that when college students engage in mindfulness meditation, they are better able to focus when met with academic anxiety or taking tests. Students found that when their minds wandered, they could more easily bring focus back to the tasks at hand (Hjeltnes et al., 2015; Kindel, 2018; Schwind et al., 2017; Stew, 2011).

Neuroscience

Some students might listen to the benefits of meditation and be thinking, *But where's the proof?* They want evidence. Discussing the neuroscience behind meditation and the brain might be a useful approach for scientific-minded students and those interested in research, such as psychology, biology, and chemistry majors. Advances in neuroscience and the ability to study what is happening in the brain of meditators have produced some fascinating findings. You might pull data and examples from various sources, such as one from *Scientific American* called "Neuroscience Reveals the Secrets of Meditation's Benefits," which details how the experience of meditation makes physiological changes in the brain.

You might mention to your students the work of Lazar and colleagues (2005), who found that the brains of meditators differed in the volume of gray matter in the insula and prefrontal cortices from that of a control group, suggesting that meditation might slow the thinning of brain tissue due to aging. In a follow-up study, the researchers demonstrated that meditation decreased the volume of the amygdala, the region associated with fear and stress response.

Creativity/Productivity

College students are slammed with studying, homework, projects, and balancing part-time jobs, sports, and extracurricular activities. Time management is often an issue. Presenting meditation as a means to boost productivity and be more creative—essentially, learning to do less and accomplish more, as their minds are more efficient, clear, and fresh—is another option. For example, a study of undergraduate students who had no previous meditation experience showed higher creativity, as evidenced by divergent thinking, than the non-meditator group (Ding et al., 2014).

A Natural Pick-Me-Up

College students need lots of energy, physical and mental, to get them through their busy schedules. Maybe the naps, coffee, energy drinks, and other strategies are not working. Meditation can give a boost of natural energy. Taking time to relax the mind-body system creates energy without the grogginess of a nap. In fact, researchers at the University of Waterloo reported that mindfulness meditation was effective for improving energy levels (Luu & Hall, 2017).

Social Intelligence and Relationships

College is a time of socializing and connecting. Take advantage of this situation by framing meditation around enhanced relationships and greater connectivity. Research suggests that meditation practice could promote greater awareness of one's feeling toward others and how those feelings shape relationships (Birnbaum, 2008; Johnson, 2016). Some students felt a greater sense of community and less alone with their stress and anxiety (Hjeltnes et al., 2015; Johnson, 2016).

Athletics

If you have student athletes in your class, then connecting meditation to sports and athletic performance might be the key. Athletes often use meditation to focus, calm the nerves, and handle the inevitable pressure that comes with competition. Long-term mindfulness meditation practice has been linked to achieving optimal athletic performance by reducing anxiety and mind wandering and increasing the experience of flow (Colzato & Kibele, 2017). Many top athletes and coaches have turned to meditation, such as Olympic champion diver Greg Louganis, who has been quoted as saying, "Peak performance is meditation in motion," and basketball star Lebron James, who apparently meditated during an actual game (https://www.youtube.com/watch?v=SCR7OfRuQd4).

Star Power

Whether we admit it or not, many of us are influenced by famous people. The average college student, being of a younger generatio,n is no exception. We can take advantage of this by telling our students about the many celebrities—actors, musicians, athletes, and businessmen and women—who practice meditation. There has been a growing number of celebrities promoting meditation and sharing their own stories. This list includes Jerry Seinfeld, Katy Perry, Oprah Winfrey, Tom Hanks, Hugh Jackman, Beyoncé, Lady Gaga, and Chris Hemsworth.

Firsthand Experience

In the meditation facilitation guide, after the students are invited to meditate and meditation is defined, the students are quickly taken through a very short sample of meditation: the ringing of the Tibetan Singing Bowl. They are asked to simply close their eyes and listen. The idea is meditation is a direct experience, a sort of first-person inquiry. Therefore, the best approach, before discussing too much about the topic, may be to lead students through an experience. This will give them context, a frame of reference, for the subjective experience of meditation. Without some experience, explaining meditation to people who have never meditated is like describing the taste of an orange to those who have never eaten one. Give your students a taste first.

A WORD ABOUT TRIGGER WARNINGS

While severe adverse reactions to various meditation techniques are rare, cases have been reported during research studies (Arias et al., 2006). It should be noted that reactions, such as during *vipassana* practice, occurred during rigorous meditation retreats. Adverse reactions include depersonalization, or confusion about a sense of self, and difficulty returning to daily life after a meditation retreat.

Nevertheless, when introducing meditation in the classroom, faculty need to consider that some individuals could have strong reactions or psychologically unpleasant experiences. For example, allowing the mind to quiet and become still can cause bad memories to arise. Meditators could become "flooded" with emotion. While this has seldom occurred in my experience with students using the meditation methods described in this book, there is the possibility (Micu, 2019), and thus, it's the facilitator's responsibility to prepare students. Having this talk should be done early in the process of implementing meditation. It is suggested that a "trigger warning" be included in course syllabi and again later discussed with students during their first experiences.

If meditation becomes too uncomfortable, the general advice is simply to stop (Thorp, 2015). This means opening the eyes and bringing the senses back to the present. Moving the body or standing up if possible can also help. The following is language that could be used or adapted to fit your syllabi:

While not always the case, when practicing meditation one may experience strong emotions, feelings, or sensations, what is known as "flooding." For this reason, you will be introduced gradually to various practices and methods under the careful guidance of the course instructor. However, if you experience flooding or a degree of discomfort at any time practicing course-related techniques either in class or at your home or dorm, please do the following:

- *Stop the practice or technique immediately.*

- *Bring your focus and awareness to the present moment by concentrating on what you are seeing, hearing, smelling, and feeling right in front of you.*
- *If possible, stand up, walk around, and shake off the body.*

IN STUDENTS' OWN WORDS

It seemed fitting to include in this chapter direct advice from students who participated in micro-meditations with actual faculty. Here are some tips that students told us during the Meditation Facilitation project, which you might keep in mind as you try these ideas with your own students:

"I think the guidance through the meditation and instruction on posture helps."

"I would say everyone's willingness to try it (helps). It has become a part of the class procedure at this point and everyone seems to enjoy it. Everyone always says how relaxed and centered they feel afterward. The sound of the singing bowl does help because it gives me something to focus on."

"Just to make a safe and quiet place for everyone and I guess to give students options when meditating."

"I would suggest not forcing them to meditate but make it voluntary."

"Have the room the way you like it—feng shui I guess you could say."

WHAT'S NEXT?

Now that you've exposed students to meditation and hopefully encouraged them to engage in it, the next step is to establish the proper environment and share the proper mindset for practice. Creating the ideal classroom setting for meditation is equally about knowing what obstacles to remove. Let's explore how to do this.

CHAPTER SUMMARY

- Invite students to join meditation practice. Avoid making them feel pressured to participate.
- Provide quiet alternative activities for students not interested in meditation.

- Define meditation and use analogies and metaphors to make the concept more relatable.
- Use various entry points to sell the benefits of and motivations to practice.
- Insert a trigger warning in your course syllabus and verbal explanations in the classroom.

Chapter 7

Setting the Stage for In-Class Meditation

While meditation can be practiced anywhere, this chapter is dedicated to turning the higher education classroom into an ideal (or mostly ideal) setting. The reality is that some classrooms simply are not the best suited for contemplative practices such as meditation. The chairs are hard or may be uncomfortable. The room might feel crowded. The lighting could be distracting, as well as the challenge of nearby noise (other students passing in the hallway, the aging air conditioning sound coming from the vent above, the landscapers outside the window).

Nevertheless, there are some actions you can take to minimize disruptions and create a more soothing environment. Faculty can also employ some props to help facilitate more calming meditation. Finally, meditator facilitators can use music, poetry, and other means to create a meditative mood. Again, tailor the suggestions in this chapter to fit your classroom.

CREATING A MEDITATIVE SPACE

What can be done to alter the classroom space so it's more conducive to meditation? In my experience, not a whole lot has to be changed to the physical layout of a classroom. The students can sit in their chairs as they normally do. The seating and tables don't necessarily have to be moved. You can experiment with, for instance, having the students sit in a circle in their chairs or form a horseshoe to create a sense of community. However, this takes time and is not necessary. Here are some suggestions that take little time or money.

Lighting

One of the simplest steps you can take to create a more soothing environment is to shut off or dim the classroom lights. Remember back in elementary school when the teacher would shut the lights off after lunch or recess before telling the students to rest their heads on their desks? Lighting impacts our moods. One note on lighting, however, is to be aware of what time of day this is done and the energy level of the students. If your class meets early in the morning or at night, perhaps keeping the lights on might work better. As one student remarked, "I feel like if we dimmed the lights at any given time in the 6:00–9:00 p.m. class I'd fall asleep because I work from 5:00 to 9:00 a.m. then come to school all day until 9:00 p.m."

Another idea for lighting that could help induce a calming tone is to place a Himalayan crystal or salt lamp in the classroom. These lamps are created by placing a light bulb inside large pieces of Himalayan salt, causing them to emit a warm, pink glow (I use one in the meditation space at the college where I work—see Chapter 10). Himalayan lamps are believed to release ions that produce health benefits into the surrounding air, but there is little research at this point to support these claims (Healthline, 2016). Nevertheless, from an aesthetic point of view, the lamps might add to the meditative atmosphere in your classroom. Experiment with the lighting and ask the students what works best for them.

Quiet Please

Talking among students was found to be one of the main hindrances to classroom meditation. It's crucial that faculty explicitly explain that the first few minutes of class time are dedicated to establishing a quiet, refreshing transition from the outside world to classroom learning. Emphasize that students who don't want to meditate can engage in one of the other silent options, and not to disturb those who make the choice to meditate.

Also consider how you will handle students arriving to class late and entering the room while meditation has begun. This can be particularly distracting for some students. Discuss with the students the procedure for this situation: They can wait outside the classroom (if you prefer) or come in quietly. Another strategy is to hang a sign outside the classroom that reads "Meditation in Progress" or "Quiet Time," which would give the students an indication of how they should proceed based on your classroom procedure. The sign would also hold off guests coming into your room unannounced.

Other Possible Ideas

These suggestions are a bit outside the box for a traditional classroom; thus, they may or may not work for your particular classroom. Incense, or a type of aromatic substance that's burned to release a fragrance, has traditionally been used to complement meditation and produce a calming state of mind. There is little scientific research on meditation and incense, but proponents claim that incense such as frankincense can reduce stress, induce relaxation, and enhance concentration. However, it should be noted that incense has been found to cause eye, throat, and nose irritation, allergic reactions, and other health complications (Scott, 2022). In addition, faculty are advised to consult campus policies regarding the use of incense and burning materials in classrooms.

Another idea that might be more pleasing to the general population is to place a small, indoor water fountain in the classroom. A small, tabletop fountain can be purchased on sites like Amazon or Wayfair for $30–40. The soothing sound of the water could serve as a calming backdrop for the students as they meditate. Used in healthcare settings, the sound of flowing water can stimulate emotions and foster a connection to the environment, which relaxes the mind (Kopec et al., 2014).

Finally, be aware of any screens that could be featured in the classroom. For instance, an overhead screen projecting a bright website or PowerPoint could be distracting, and you may want to shut off the screen. Other technology in the classroom, such as a desktop computer, could be making a humming sound.

Addressing Technology

A major consideration in creating the proper environment and assisting students in taking some time to mentally recharge prior to instruction is the handling of their technological devices. It's highly likely that when you begin meditation, some (or maybe all) students will be using their laptop computers and/or cellular phones. When conducting the Meditation Facilitation project, faculty asked the students to put aside their devices for a few minutes to engage in meditation or another mind-recharging activity.

You might say something like, "Let's give our devices a rest while we give our minds a rest." Of course, whether the students use technology during this time is entirely your call. One exception might be allowing students to softly listen to music.

If time permits, you could cite research suggesting that excessive technology use and screen time could have negative effects, including reduced attention, impaired emotional and social intelligence, technology addiction, social isolation, and sleep deprivation (Small et al., 2022). For example, in one study involving adolescents without symptoms of attention deficit hyperactivity disorder (ADHD) at the start of the study suggested significant association between frequent use of digital media and ADHD symptoms after 24 months (Ra et al., 2018).

Using Props

Certain props, or supports, can be used to aid the meditative experience. One is the use of sound, as created by bells, singing bowls, or chimes. The Meditation Project facilitators used Tibetan Singing Bowls, which the majority of students found extremely helpful. The bowls, which can be purchased for as low as $10–20 on Amazon, trace back to about 2000 BC in Asia. The handheld bowls, at least traditionally, were made of an alloy of various types, such as copper and tin. The bowls were used for cooking, playing music, and complementing meditation practices. If a singing bowl feels too "non-secular" for the classroom, some meditation teachers may opt to use a chime, which can also be bought cheaply online.

While the students may enjoy the soothing sounds, there is science behind the use of the singing bowl or bell. Historically, sound has been used in ancient wisdom traditions to facilitate meditation, affect mental states, and induce healing (Goldsby, et al., 2017; Jansen, 1990; Schussel & Miller, 2013). The use of a bowl has been scientifically investigated as a vehicle to align the brain with a meditative state (see, e.g., Cahn & Polich, 2006; Inácio et al., 2006; Jansen 1992; Schussel & Miller, 2013). Researchers have determined that, when played at one revolution per second, the singing bowl "may cause neural entrainment influencing a deep meditative state due to the resonant effect of the bowl causing 4–6 beats per revolution, the equivalence of REM cycle number 1, Theta" (Goldsby et al., 2016, 83).

Listening to the sound of various bowls can decrease feelings of tension and anxiety, particularly with more impact on those new to the experience (Goldsby et al., 2016). Essentially, just having the students listen to a soothing vibration in itself can help calm the nerves and prepare the mind. As one student stated, "I like the singing bowl. It's like a switch that changes the intention and allows for calmness to enter the space."

To create the right mood or vibe, try ringing the bowl or chime before *vipassana* as a mental warm-up. Ask the students to listen to the sound as they would music they enjoy, without evaluating. Then, you can proceed to guide them through the watching of the breath or another meditation technique. If time is short, the bowl or chime *can be a brief meditation*. Just ring it and have the students listen, then proceed with business as usual.

CREATING THE MEDITATIVE MINDSET

In addition to creating a supportive environment, part of setting the stage for meditation in the classroom is guiding the students in adopting the proper mindset. How they mentally approach meditation—their attitude—makes all the difference. Meditation is not meant to be a serious affair or hard work. Meditation is relaxing into oneself. Rather than swimming upstream, meditation is a let-go. It's floating downriver on a tube, going with the current.

Thus, encourage the students to approach meditation playfully, lightly, and with a sense of ease and relaxation. Promote the practice ("practice" might not even be the correct word) as an opportunity to rest, to "chill" as students might say—a chance to unwind, to center, and to just "be." The following tips can help create this mood.

Music

Perhaps play some calming or uplifting music as the students come into the classroom and prepare to meditate (you will want to turn the music off when meditating). A quick YouTube search of "calming music," "meditation music," or "Zen music" will produce some tracks; however, you can use other types of music that will get your students in a playful, celebrative, relaxed state.

Poetry

To create a meditative atmosphere, try reciting poetry right before starting meditation. Basho, the Japanese poet and Haiku master who lived in the 1600s, crafted some perfect poems, including:

> *An ancient pond*
> *A frog jumps in*
> *Splash! Silence again*

And:

> *Sitting quietly*
> *Doing nothing*
> *Spring comes*
> *And the grass grows by itself*

Other meditative muses include Walt Whitman, Rumi, and the contemporary poet Rupi Kaur. Maybe share her work titled "Be Here":

I get so lost
In where I want to go
I forget that the place I'm in
Is already quite magical

Humor

If you are prone to telling jokes or sharing funny stories, laughter provides the perfect mindset to meditate. Laughter is similar to meditation in the sense that one is relaxed and completely present in the moment. As Dove (2017) wrote,

> Laughter gives you a glimpse of freedom from the mind. For those moments when you are totally laughing, you are free of the mind. All your problems disappear for a few seconds, don't they? You cannot think and laugh at the same time. In those moments when you are out of the mind, you are in meditation. (n.p.)

Relaxation

Asking people to sit quietly and fall into a relaxed state of consciousness can be difficult if they are tense. Thus, guiding the students in a relaxation technique can also prep them for meditation. Progressive relaxation involves intentionally tightening a muscle and then relaxing it. You can have the students engage in an abridged version. First, ask the students to tense their toes, feet, and legs for five seconds (without straining or hurting themselves, of course), then release. Then have them tense their stomach, back, arms, and hands, then release. Finally, ask them to tighten their shoulders, neck, and facial muscles and release. This adds a few minutes to the meditation activity, but it could assist the students in meditation practice and de-stressing before class.

TIERS OF IMPLEMENTATION

Before getting into specifically how to facilitate, you may want to ponder how involved—meaning how much time, energy, and intensity you want to invest in meditation in the classroom—and reflect on the current needs of your students. To serve as a framework for implementation, including to what degree and intensity you incorporate meditation in the classroom, the following tier system was created.

Tier 1

This first level could involve simply asking the students when they first enter the room to sit quietly. You might also ring a bell or chime and invite them to listen, then move on. This approach would be the least time-consuming—no instruction in an actual meditation technique, no in-depth explanations, no advancing the activity. Perhaps you are comfortable trying something like David Borker, a professor of accounting and management at Manhattan College, uses. On the first day of class, he gives these instructions:

I would like you to consider a short practice we could do at the beginning and end of class that involves ringing a bell like this one three times *[rings bell once]*. Some students have found that it helps them to reduce stress and focus better during the class. Would you be interested in trying it out for a while? (see Owen-Smith, 2018, p. 32)

The beauty of this tier system is its fluid. So you might want to remain at Tier 1, which is perfectly fine, as you find it serves your students well. However, in a subsequent semester, you may become motivated, based on your early results, to advance to Tier 2 or even 3 (then you would want to closely consult the protocol in Chapter 9).

Tier 2

This tier becomes more involved (and takes more time) since it requires teaching the students a specific meditation technique, such as *vipassana* or the body scan. Faculty would begin on the first day of class, explaining the benefits of meditation, and select some entry points (Chapter 6) to hook the students. In the first few weeks, they would move toward facilitating the meditation technique, providing guidance, and maybe allowing some time or ways for the students to share their experiences. What differentiates this from Tier 3 is that you would not go into detailed explanations of the technique, including the neuroscience behind it, and would forgo sharing any meditation extension activities (found in Chapter 8). You simply teach the students a technique and stick with it for the semester.

Tier 3

At this tier, you're "all in." You might start class with simply a bell listening activity, but then you strategically move to facilitating a breath meditation technique, and once the students grasp it, advancing to other meditative

Table 7.1. Meditation in the Classroom Implementation Tiers

Tier	Characteristics
1	Least time-consuming Brief explanation/facilitation Inviting the students to a moment of silence or Ringing a bell or chime and asking them to listen
2	Requires more explanation/use of entry points Facilitation is more involved Teaching specific meditation technique(s)
3	Most time-consuming of the tiers Facilitation and explanation more intensive Use of entry points, definitions, and analogies of meditation Possible sharing of meditation experiences Advancing meditation beyond original technique by sharing extension activities

activities. The protocol in Chapter 9 will be indispensable. Table 7.1 outlines the tiers and their characteristics.

Note: Regardless of what tier you fall within, it's still highly recommended that you give the students various options if they don't want to participate in these activities (revisit Chapter 6 for suggestions).

WHAT'S NEXT?

With the ability to establish the ideal classroom environment for meditation, it's time to proceed to actual facilitation of meditation techniques with the students. The next chapter will cover considerations such using the proper tone of voice and how much to talk when facilitating. You will also learn how to extend the meditation practice by introducing various activities outside of *vipassana* and mindfulness meditation.

CHAPTER SUMMARY

- Create a classroom environment conducive to meditation by adjusting the lighting and working to eliminate distractions.
- Use props such as a singing bowl or a chime to help warm the mind up for meditation.
- Generate a meditation mood prior to practice using music, poetry, or humor.
- Reflect on what *tier of implementation* best suits your classroom.

Chapter 8

Advancing the Meditation

Now that you have learned how to introduce brief meditation to your students and create an ideal environment, it's time to facilitate. In this chapter, we will cover specifically how to guide the students through *vipassana* and other mindfulness meditation methods, providing examples and advice. In addition, you will learn how to keep the momentum going by including other meditative enhancements and activities throughout the semester.

GUIDING STUDENTS THROUGH MEDITATION

While the entire facilitation guide can be accessed in Chapter 9, let's walk through a few examples of facilitating a meditation with students and study how you can build upon their experiences. Imagine it's the first week of the semester. You have shared with the students a clear definition of meditation, and depending on the makeup of your class (their individual goals and challenges, fields of study, etc.), provided a compelling rationale. Maybe you hang a "Meditation in Progress" sign outside your classroom door. Then, you can follow these steps:

1. Say: "I'd like to *invite* you to put away your technology for a minute. Let's give the mind a brief rest by giving our phones and laptops a rest."
2. Say: "I'm going to turn off or dim the lights, just so it helps create a calming atmosphere."
3. Say: "This is a Tibetan Singing Bowl (or a chime), which is used sometimes in meditation. It produces a pleasant vibration, which can help focus and soothe the mind and body. I'm going to ring the bowl (or chime), and I'd like you to simply listen to the sound as it drops off. You can also listen to 'what remains' after the sound of the bowl disappears."

4. Say: "It may help to sit upright. Have your feet planted on the floor. You can let your hands rest easily in your lap. If you are comfortable, it may help to close your eyes, or you can softly cast them downward."
5. Ring the bowl or chime.
6. Wait about 30 seconds to a minute after the sound of the bowl fades away. Then, instruct students to "gradually" come out of the meditation by slowly opening their eyes and blinking them if that helps. They can stretch the body.

After having the students listen to the chime or bowl for the first week of classes, you can move to inviting them to engage in *vipassana*. Again, after briefly discussing meditation and rationale (or you could skip this part), it would look like this:

1. Say: "I'd like to again *invite* everyone to participate in a short meditation. However, this time, we are going to practice what is known as mindfulness breath meditation, or *vipassana*, which originates from the Buddhist tradition but has been implemented in many facets of Western society, such as education, business, sports, counseling, and the medical field.

   With this method, we listen to the sound of the bowl but then gently turn our attention to the natural flow of the in-breath and out-breath. We can think of 'watching' or 'witnessing' the breath in its natural state. The key is to not manipulate the breath or 'try to make something happen'; rather, we are 'dropping in' on what is already happening and being mindful of 'what is.'"

   Finally, it's important to bring a nonjudgmental attitude and kind awareness to your practice of meditation. *The ideal attitude toward meditation is one of playfulness or being easy and relaxed about it— this allows the meditation to happen.*
2. Say: "Sit with your back straight but not stiff. Have your feet planted on the floor. Allow your hands to rest easily in your lap, either cupped or with palms facing up. Allow your eyes to close or softly look downward. Notice, just by the way you are seated, if you can sense a feeling of centeredness and presence. If not, see if slightly adjusting your posture helps."
3. Ring the bowl or chime.
4. After the sound begins to fade, say: "Now, gently turn your attention to the breath as it flows in and out. There is a natural rhythm to the breath. Just observe or listen to this rhythm." As the facilitator, sit quietly and observe the students. Allow a minute or two—or whatever time you can—for them to meditate.

5. Say: "I'm going to ring the bowl (or chime) as a way to indicate that the meditation is ending. Please take your time coming out of the meditation." Instruct the students to *gradually* come out of the meditation by slowly opening their eyes, blinking them if that helps. They can stretch the body.

Optional: At this point, you can address how to handle thoughts and distractions during meditation or wait further into the semester, after the students have more experience. You might say:

Did anyone have any thoughts or become distracted during the meditation? This is completely natural. There is a misconception that meditation involves completely clearing the mind of thoughts. Trying to stop or eliminate thoughts is like trying to stop your heart from beating. If we are patient, however, and simply witness our thoughts passing, in time they begin to slow down.

In meditation, we bring a nonjudgmental, open attitude to thoughts—meaning, if we have thoughts or become distracted from the breath, it's *no big deal*. If at any time we become lost in thought or unfocused, we can very easily return to the breath. Meditation is very much of a process of remembering the breath and returning our awareness to it.

(MORE ON) HOW LONG STUDENTS SHOULD MEDITATE

This is the million-dollar question. There is not an exact recommendation for how long students should spend in meditation. When developing the meditation facilitation guide, faculty spent as little as oneto four or five minutes before proceeding with class. Based on student feedback, the results in terms of helping them focus and de-stress were consistent—the variation of a minute or two didn't make a real difference. Consider factors such as how much time you can afford before "dipping" into the academic content. For example, if the class meets for only one hour, limiting the meditation to a minute or two might be prudent. However, the class is three hours long, you could begin with a three-to-four-minute meditation or maybe start class with a two-minute meditation and then invite the students to engage in a second two-minute meditation during the half-time break.

In the beginning, the meditation activity will naturally take more class time as you explain the background, advise the students on how to sit, and guide them through the technique, but then the whole experience can be streamlined as the students gain experience.

SOME NOTES ON THE ROLE OF THE FACILITATOR

The role of the facilitator in meditation with students is "essential" (Shonin et al., 2013, p. 856). You essentially can make or break the activity (no pressure, right?). Research with meditation and college students discovered that "the face-to-face exercise was more effective" (Shonin et al., 2013, p. 856) since students preferred a personal connection with the facilitator. Furthermore, "tone of voice and pacing" (Lauricella, 2013, p. 685) and the authenticity of the instructor had a major impact on the appeal of participation (Kindel, 2018; Schwind et al., 2017). Let's dive more into these areas.

Face-to-Face Facilitation

If you teach a class in person, this is an easy one. Facilitate directly with the students if possible (as opposed to utilizing a video of you or someone else guiding the meditation). This also goes for a hybrid class—facilitate when the class meets in person. If you teach strictly online, try to facilitate "live."

Your Voice and Tone Matter

When verbalizing instructions, the tone of your voice and your overall delivery really matter. In surveys, students repeatedly noted how the course instructor's voice and presence helped prepare them to meditate. As one put it, "the instructor's facilitation of the meditation is very helpful because the instructor has a very calming voice that truly allows you to calm and really get in meditation."

This means faculty must be cognizant of their energy and stress levels prior to facilitation. Perhaps a brief meditation in your office before class could put you in the proper frame of mind. Establishing a personal meditation practice (as this book strongly advises) would support coaching others. Another suggestion is to record yourself facilitating parts of the guide and then listen back to it to hear how you might come across to the students. Initially, you may have to read the guide language to the students until you familiarize yourself with it. Over time, the facilitation will become more natural.

How Much Should You Talk?

This is also nuanced. You obviously must do some talking as you guide the students through meditation, particularly when first starting. However, you must be mindful of how talking might impact the students' experience. As one student wrote in her feedback survey: "I feel that the interruptions throughout the meditation (guiding us what to think about, telling us to think of what our relationships were with the people around us) were distracting and not very beneficial." The advice for how much you should speak when students are in meditation is generally *less is more*. As students gain more experience, gently ease up on how much talking you do. In the guide, you will notice that any speaking occurs *before* and *after* the meditation. Give the students quiet time to explore their inner worlds.

Authenticity

Be real with the students in terms of guiding them through the meditation, reading parts if the script if you must. Be transparent about your own concerns and anxieties with practicing and teaching meditation. This advice worked well for faculty who experimented with facilitation in their classrooms. They openly expressed their thoughts and feelings around meditation as well as their efforts to improve how they facilitate.

HAVING STUDENTS SHARE EXPERIENCES

Another question that may come up is, *Should you have students share their experiences with meditation?* Having the students compare notes about their meditation experiences could assist classmates. For example, a student might mention how they had a lot of thoughts running through their mind or that meditation was not particularly peaceful because they were having a difficult day or week. Other students might realize that this was also their experience, they are not alone, and not all meditation sessions are blissful. One challenge is that any sharing of experiences eats into additional class instruction. Also be advised that meditation is a very personalized experience, and some students simply don't want to share. Thus, this should *always* be optional. The following strategies allow the students to share their meditation experiences confidentially or in safe spaces.

Turn and Talk

Have the students turn to a classmate and share their meditation experience (of course, make it voluntary). Provide prompts such as, "Share with a classmate if you had lots of thoughts during your meditation today and how you dealt with them," or "Share whether you found meditation easy today and what challenges you might have had." In this way, students can learn from each other.

Reflective Journal

This strategy enables the students to share their experiences strictly with you. Have the students write a one- or two-paragraph description of their experience with meditation, perhaps once during midsemester and once at the end of the semester. Another approach is to invite students to record a brief video (for example, educational platforms such as Canvas now have video-recording features). They can post the reflection as an ungraded assignment.

Here is an excerpt from a student journal after the students were asked to journal for a week while meditating in class:

Day 1: Sitting still for 10 minutes was the toughest thing in meditation. After five minutes, my legs started to feel numb and my concentration kept fading away. Breathing is what we do without even realizing, but I could not breathe well when I tried to focus on my breathing. I had difficulty even hearing the sound of my breath. Another thing I realized was that something that never bothers me could really bother me during the meditation. Sounds of people talking, noise of my neighbors, things in nature caused distraction for me during the meditation. The more I tried to focus, the more I became distracted. That was difficult. I also kept focusing on getting it right, but I just got myself more tense. I also decided to lie down during meditation tomorrow. That might help with concentration and make me more relaxed.

Day 2: During the meditation, I thought of how I could improve my concentration during the meditation. I know that meditation helps to purify the mind, but only disturbing thoughts came up during the meditation. I couldn't shut off the thoughts of what was to come next. I just remembered what we did in class and I focused on the "bell" in my mind. I believe this is a necessary practice in life. I figured out that I need to start small with a small amount of time and then move up. Overall meditation gives me time to be aware and present in my feelings and thoughts.

I don't feel pain with sitting anymore, although sometimes I start thinking and cannot focus on being empty and my mind moves around, but that's okay. Five minutes passes more quickly than before. I'm not looking at the time to see how long I've been meditating. It may just be my imagination, but I feel I'm able to center myself better.

Day 3: My attitude toward meditation has become positive; it's no longer negative. I was willing to start to meditate to find out what kind of outcome I would receive out of this session. Once I started to meditate, I realized how clear my mind was. To be honest, I was not thinking about anything during the meditation. I was not enjoying the moment or hating the moment. I was neutral. When I opened up my eyes and checked how long I had been meditating, I found out that I was meditating for 10 minutes without any thoughts. That's a big accomplishment.

Lying down is very relaxing for me. I placed the pillow behind my head and I'm able to focus on my breathing more. I could control it better than before. I'm beginning to look forward to the next session of meditation. I decided to meditate again tonight before bed. This gave me time to decompress from the day. I have learned that meditation gives me the opportunity to face myself when I become deflated or have an anxiety. At times like that, I usually tend to escape from the matter and try to get them away from my mind, though I have learned the importance of facing my problems, not turning away from them.

Day 4: Great session today. My attention didn't waver too much, though I did have to reset my breathing twice during my practice. What I realized is that when you enter the heart. The love that is always dwelling there is the love for yourself. It seems that we often shy away from going inside because we have conditioned ourselves to fear intimacy and fear love. Our higher selves are always right there ready to be embraced fully. However, something in us kind of wants pain. Maybe it's because we don't want to make ourselves too vulnerable and feel an even deeper pain. And this too translates to our relationship with ourselves. We don't want to go inside and then let ourselves down. In meditation today I realized that because I already love myself, I can love myself even deeper and fuller and more beautifully than I realized. Because I AM love and so are you. And because you are love, what you feel in your heart during meditation is seeing through the veil. I have thought how I wish there was a better word to embody that.

Fielding Questions from Students

Once you begin facilitating meditation, students will naturally have questions about their experiences. This beckons the importance of first establishing your own practice to gain firsthand knowledge and experience so you can relate (see Chapter 4). However, it's difficult to know exactly what meditators will ask and on what points they will want more clarification or elaboration. Thus, the following section outlines some possible questions that students might ask and how you might respond.

Is It Typical to Have Lots of Thoughts during Meditation?

Answer: The mind is always thinking, projecting to the future or going back to the past. So yes, it's perfectly normal to have thoughts when meditating. Sometimes, your mind will be very busy and you will have many thoughts. Other times when meditating, you might have fewer thoughts or, in some cases, glimpses of what is called "no-mind," or having no thoughts for that moment.

My Meditation Didn't Feel Good Today—How Come?

Answer: Your experience in meditation will vary. Sometimes it might feel very good, even blissful, while on other days it might feel "rougher" or not so pleasant. Your mind and body are in different states or conditions depending on the day or time, so meditation experiences are unique. For example, if you are stressed and tense on a particular day, the meditation might feel different than meditating when relaxed, say, on the beach during vacation. Just stay regular with the meditation; you can still experience benefits in your daily life even if the actual meditation experience wasn't the best feeling.

I Noticed My Breathing Slowed Down or Deepened When Meditating—Is This Okay?

Answer: This is good! Often, when doing a meditation such as *vipassana*, the breath will naturally slow down or deepen on its own. This is an indication that you are relaxing and activating the parasympathetic nervous system—the opposite of the stress or fight-or-flight response.

Is It Okay to Experience Seeing Lights, Colors, or Visions, Feeling Sensations in the Body, Etc.?

Answer: Each meditation experience is unique to the individual. You might experience seeing lights or colors or feeling various sensations. As long as it's comfortable, then continue with the meditation.

How Do I Know This Stuff Is Working?

Answer: Good question! You might notice some immediate benefit during or after meditation; for example, you may feel more relaxed or a sense of calm or peace after meditating. Also look for signs that the meditation is working in your daily life. Maybe you don't get angry as quickly or as often; have more clarity and focus in your academic studies, work, and personal life; or feel more energy. Maybe your relationships are enhanced. Maybe you laugh more, just feel better about your life in general, have a greater feeling of well-being. Since meditation is so individualized, it's impossible to pinpoint exactly what the benefits will be for each person.

The Meditation Doesn't Work for Me—Am I Doing It Wrong?

Answer: Not necessarily. If you have followed the directions in class and given it some time, then perhaps this particular meditation is not appropriate or does not suit you best at this time. We can discuss other meditation methods and techniques. We will also be engaging in other meditation approaches later in the semester, and you may find one that clicks better.

MEDITATIVE EXTENSION ACTIVITIES

In itself, *vipassana* meditation or a simple mindfulness listening meditation is enough for the classroom. Faculty could invite the students to participate in these meditation methods at the start of each class. Nevertheless, it has been my and colleague's experience that, while beneficial, using the same approach in each class can become routine, and mixing it up can maintain interest and momentum. The idea is to give students a foundation, perhaps four to six weeks with meditation techniques described in Chapter 4. From there, you can experiment with varying meditation methods and add activities that include movement. In some cases, these activities, such as Zen Doodling, could serve as alternatives for students not wanting to engage in the daily guided meditation. The following are some suggestions for extension activities.

Loving-Kindness Meditation

This meditation method, known as *metta*, is from the Buddhist tradition. This meditation aims to intentionally generate feelings of warmth for oneself and others. While instructions vary, here is an abridged version you can practice with students:

1. Assume a comfortable position (as instructed with *vipassana* and other meditation methods in this book).
2. Bring one's attention to the heart/chest area, observing the natural rhythm of the breath.
3. Gently and silently repeat the following phrases: *May I be happy. May I be well. May I be safe. May I be peaceful.*
4. If time permits, bring to mind a person who brings you joy or happiness. Imagine they are sitting across from you. Use the same phrases as above, but direct the feelings of loving-kindness toward this person. For instance, *may you be happy. May you be well.*

5. Allow yourself to feel what is occurring in the heart area—for instance, any pleasant feelings of love, happiness, caring, or well-being. Slowly open your eyes.

Meditative Spoon Activities

These exercises get students moving while requiring a meditative mindset. During the first one, set up bowls of water on each side of the classroom or place them in a hallway or outdoors if possible. Provide each student with a plastic spoon. Instruct them that they must carefully take a spoonful of water from a bowl and carry it to another bowl across the room (or hall or courtyard) without spilling it. They then take another spoonful from the second bowl and bring it to the first bowl. Afterward, ask them about their mindset: *Were you focused on anything in particular? Was your focus narrowed on the spoon but also aware of your surroundings? Did you move slower or faster? Were you able to think, talk, or be on your cell phones?* The debriefing prompts them to reflect on being able to be meditative while in action. A second activity involves giving the students a spoon and having them form a circle while standing.

A student is instructed to take a spoonful of water and then pass it to the classmate to their right (or left, it doesn't matter). The students must try to pass the water without spilling any drops as they go around the entire circle. This activity develops a meditative, focused mindset but also builds collaboration. Again, you can debrief with the students by asking them about their experience with the mindful spoon circle activity and what they noticed about their minds during the process.

Zen Doodling

Students can sketch or doodle as a form of artistic meditation. This doodling activity taps into their creativity while promoting a calm, focused state of mind. Zentangle (zentangle.com) is an intricate approach to doodling with a meditative mindset. The site provides detailed instructions and resources to get started. The following is an abridged version of meditation doodling that can be completed in just a few minutes at the start of class:

1. Give the students a blank piece of paper.
2. Ask them to draw three circles (the shapes need to be large enough to doodle inside of them).

3. Tell them that when you hit the meditation bell or chime, they are to silently create patterns inside the circles. The patterns can be anything they want. Once they finish one circle, they continue making patterns in the next circle.
4. Encourage them to *listen* to the sound of the pencil or pen as it moves across the paper, to feel how the writing instrument *feels* in their hand, to closely observe how the shapes take form. If they lose attention, they gently bring their awareness back to the doodling.
5. Ring the bell or chime again to have the students stop doodling.

Meditation Poem

A variation on breath meditation that has worked well with college students is to share with them a poem by Zen Master Thich Nhat Hanh, which links simple phrases to the rhythm of the breath (Hanh, 1998). Hanh abbreviates the concept that the breath goes *in* and *out,* which causes it to become *deep* and *slow,* producing a sense of *calm* and *ease.* When you breathe in now from this relaxed place, you can *smile* and *release* and you realize this *present moment* is a *wonderful moment.*

To engage in this meditation, have the students sit in the usual posture, then ask them to close their eyes or look downward and become aware of the breath. Then, guide them on silently saying these phrases in conjunction with the flow of the breath:

> *In (as the breath flows in)*
> *Out (as the breath moves out)*
> *Deep (as the breath flows in)*
> *Slow (as the breath moves out)*
> *Calm (as the breath flows in)*
> *Ease (as the breath moves out)*
> *Smile (as the breath flows in)*
> *Release (as the breath moves out)*
> *Present moment (as the breath flows in)*
> *Wonderful moment (as the breath moves out)*

Depending on available time and the students' experience levels, you could shorten the meditation to something like:

> *In*
> *Out*
> *Calm*
> *Ease*

Eating Meditation

To add a fun twist, you can have the students engage in meditation using food. Again, there are varying instructions for this meditation. The idea is to use all the senses and consume food in a slower, more aware fashion. For more detailed instructions, check out Script-Mindful-Eating.pdf (va.gov) or Mindful-Eating-Transcript.pdf (dukehealth.org). Since these activities will likely take more than a few minutes, the following is an abridged version for your classroom:

1. Pass out a food item to the students, such as a piece of chocolate, a raisin, an apple slice, or a gummy bear. It might be good to offer students a choice (also check with them for any food allergies).
2. Ask the students to hold the piece of food in their hands, briefly being mindful of the shape and texture. Encourage them to look closely at the item.
3. Have them bring the item near their nose and, closing their eyes, smell the food. Tell them to be aware of how this impacts the mouth and the stomach—does it bring up any sensations, any memories?
4. Next, invite the students to place the food in their mouths without chewing it. Direct them to hold it in their mouths for 10 seconds, being aware of their tastebuds and the sensations that arise in the mind and body. Tell them to chew the item slowly, being aware of the sensations and flavors as they move their mouths.
5. Finally, instruct them to bring awareness to how the food moves down the throat and toward the stomach when they swallow.
6. If time permits, you can debrief the students with questions such as: What was your experience with eating in this manner? What did you notice about using your senses—were you aware of anything new or that you normally didn't notice when eating? Did any particular thoughts or memories pop up?

Warrior's Meditation

Richard Haight (2020), martial arts instructor and meditation teacher, teaches a form of meditation that moves past simply using the breath or a mantra. Rather, this meditation approach, a natural state he believes our ancestral hunter-gatherers experienced, relies on using all the senses to reach an open, relaxed state of awareness. Here are the essential steps:

1. Take several breaths, gently holding the air and moving it around the lungs where it feels best, then releasing.

2. Bring awareness to the total visual field (this includes anything in your peripheral).
3. Notice any sound, near or far.
4. Notice the sense of smell and the feeling of the breath in the nasal passages.
5. Pay attention to the sense of taste and any feelings in the mouth.
6. Become aware of the entire body and any physical sensations.
7. Notice the space around the body.

Walking Meditation

Another extension that provides movement to the meditative experience is walking meditation. This provides an alternative to students who might find sitting and meditating difficult. The following method can be completed in under five minutes:

1. Meet with the students in an area where walking freely can occur. This could be a hallway near the classroom or outside the building, in the campus quad or courtyard. It's conducive, but not necessary, to do walking meditation near natural elements such as trees, grass, or lakes.
2. Inform the students that they are going to engage in a walking meditation (of course, this is an invitation, so provide other options such as quietly listening to music, doing a sitting meditation, or doodling). Require them to walk alone, without talking to classmates, and put their cell phones or other technological devices away so they can be present in the moment.
3. Instruct the students that when you hit the bowl or chime, they will select a personal path to walk and begin walking slowly in that direction. Demonstrate how when they walk, they will bring their awareness to how the bottom of the heel meets the ground every time they take a step. Guide them to pay attention to their natural breathing as they walk, as well as their senses, to observe movement (such as the birds flying, a squirrel scurrying up a tree, how the leaves blow in the wind), to listen closely (to the sound of traffic, to the wind, etc.), and to feel (the sunshine on their skin or the temperature outside).
4. Tell them that they will walk for about a minute or two in this way, and when you ring the bell or chime, they will walk back meditatively.

Meditation in Motion (Tai Chi, Qigong, Yoga)

Continuing the theme of meditation movement, you might have students engage in martial arts, including Tai Chi or Qigong, which rely on slow-motion movements and sequences, or yoga, which uses intentional poses to synchronize mind, body, and awareness. Several studies suggest that college students experience positive moods and health benefits from practicing Tai Chi (Caldwell et al., 2009). Yoga has also been found to be beneficial to college-age students, helping to reduce stress and anxiety (see, e.g., Lemay et al., 2019; Villate, 2015). Invite local instructors of these traditions to come speak and your students and, depending on the time available, demonstrate some movements. Often, college and universities will already have experienced instructors offering classes and workshops on campus, who can serve as guest facilitators.

Visualization

Asking students to visualize—or use mental imagery—can be a powerful supplement to their meditation. Visualization, which has been used by Olympic and professional athletes for years, in itself has demonstrated many benefits, including improved performance, decreased stress, and enhanced well-being and health. A YouTube search can yield various visualization meditations and exercise. In addition, the apps listed in Chapter 4 can provide resources and ideas you can use with students. Here is an abridged visualization you can try (Osho, 1974):

Imagine you are lying on your back, floating down a tranquil river that passes between two mountains. You are completely relaxed, enjoying the experience. You have completely let go, allowing yourself to be taken by the current. Bring all your senses into the experience—hear the current move, the birds chirping, feel the breeze on your face, the warmth of the sun, see the bright colors of the mountain landscape, the shapes of the clouds.

See yourself float onto a riverbank. You are lying on the sand and feel yourself completely disintegrate. Each body part evaporates as you are completely relaxed, enjoying the process. As you disaggregate into the atmosphere, continue to look around at the water, the sky, the mountains. Hear the birds, see the dolphins playing in the surf. Feel your awareness or presence still there, though your body has disappeared. When ready, slowly open your eyes.

The Pulse Rate Experiment

This activity requires more equipment and expense but demonstrates visible evidence that even short meditation can have an impact. Hand out heart rate monitors or fingertip pulse oximeters to the students. Ask them to check their resting pulse before meditating (the average resting pulse for adults is 60–100 beats per minute) and write down the number. Then, after engaging in one of the brief meditation techniques suggested in this book, have them check their pulse rates again. They may find that their pulse rates go down, even just after a few minutes. You can purchase a fingertip pulse oximeter for as low as \$12–13 on Amazon or for a similar price at Walmart or other stores that sell medical devices. Another idea is to check on campus—for example, with the nursing program or medical college—to see if you can borrow monitors.

WHAT'S NEXT?

In the next chapter, the meditation facilitation guide will be presented in its entirety. Armed with a foundation of the concept of meditation, how to establish the proper environment, andhandle distractions and other challenges, and knowledge of how to move the meditation experience along, you are ready for detailed notes regarding facilitation. The guide suggests specific phrases and language that you can use with your students throughout the entire process, and gives a road map for implementing meditation during the course of a semester.

CHAPTER SUMMARY

- Give the students thorough but brief meditation practice, finding the appropriate pace.
- Be intentional about the tone of your voice (create a calming presence) and the amount of time you speak.
- Continue the momentum of the practice by introducing meditation extension activities.

Chapter 9

The Meditation Facilitation Guide

You made it. You've demonstrated a commitment to being innovative, to trying something different in your college or university classroom, and to helping students with stress and increased distractions. You have studied meditation and, hopefully, tried the methods detailed in this book. You've been guided on how to create a supportive environment and contemplated the challenges you will face. Now, it's time to get into the logistics of facilitation, to see what meditation in the classroom can look like—the phrasing, the sequencing, the pacing.

The facilitation guide below was developed by faculty members working together on the project during the 2021–2022 academic year. Each professor implemented meditation at the start of their classes using a guide that I developed. That original document was based on my 25 years of experience with meditation, including teaching students and others. Based on the experiences of the faculty team who piloted brief meditation in their classrooms and feedback from their students, the guide was refined to improve the facilitation process. The end result was a road map that any course instructor can use, regardless of their field of study or the campus where they teach.

But remember, a theme of this book is to make this knowledge your own. Review this guide, memorize it, and implement it, but by all means, adapt and improve it to meet your students' needs. The guide is segmented into eight days—or eight classes—of facilitation, modeling a detailed account of what to do on each of those days. After that, instructors can maintain the meditation protocol or, as Chapter 8 suggests, add enhancements by introducing new activities and methods. To assist with planning, the guide also notes the expected time each meditation activity will take (of course, these are estimates).

MEDITATION FACILITATION GUIDE

Day 1

(Total time: 2–3 minutes)

Prior to class, you may want to hang a sign on the door saying "Meditation in Progress: Please Wait Outside" for late students (or tell the students at the start of the semester that if the door is closed, come in quietly). Also consider closing the door, shutting off any technology (overhead projectors, etc.), and dimming the lights, as this can help create a meditative atmosphere and reduce distractions.

After the students enter the classroom, begin the facilitation by saying:

Before we start the class and engage in learning, I'd like to *invite* everyone to participate in a brief meditation. Meditation is a way of settling into oneself, touching in with our center. While there are many misconceptions about meditation, meditation is simply a process of watching or witnessing the mind. We might think of our thoughts like clouds and the meditative mind like the sky. If we simply observe our thoughts with nonjudgment, they tend to slow down and have less power. We gain a sense of clarity and connectedness. But, as you might have noticed, our minds can be quite busy! Lots of things pass through the mind. While based within various traditions, meditation methods can be practiced as nonreligious, secular techniques and methods to help with stress, anxiety, and other challenges. For example, we can observe the natural flow of the breath as it comes in and out. We can also use sound. Today, we will try a short listening meditation.

(*Note:* This approach relies on encouraging meditation to assist with clarity and focus and to reduce stress. Chapter 5 outlines different entry points based on your student population.)

However, I want to be clear that meditating in class is completely voluntary and there's no requirement to practice. You can think of this as quiet reflection time before we start learning new content. If you choose, you can listen to music quietly, engage in prayer, reflect, or sketch or draw, whatever you decide. During the next few classes, I will share some other specific activities you can try to relax the mind. Regardless of your choice, we must maintain a quiet environment for the next few minutes—so please no talking, no loud music, etc.

Then, go through the following instructions for the actual meditation technique:

1. Say: "I'd like to invite you to put away your technology for a minute. Let's give the mind a brief rest by giving our phones and laptops a rest. I'm going to turn off or dim the lights, just so it helps create a calming atmosphere."
2. Say: "This is a Tibetan Singing Bowl (or chime), which is used sometimes in meditation. It produces a pleasant vibration, which can help focus and soothe the mind and body. I'm going to ring the bowl, and I'd like you to simply listen to the sound as it drops off. You can also listen to 'what remains' after the sound of the bowl disappears."
3. Say: "It may help to sit upright. Have your feet planted on the floor. You can let your hands rest easily in your lap. If you are comfortable, it may help to close your eyes, or you can cast them downward."
4. Ring the bowl or chime.
5. Wait about 30 seconds to a minute after the sound of the bowl fades away. Then, instruct the students to "gradually" come out of the meditation by slowly opening their eyes, blinking them if that helps. They can stretch the body.

Day 2

(Total time: 2–3 minutes)

Repeat the script from Day 1, slightly adjusting since you have already introduced the practice.

Prior to class, you may want to hang a sign on the door saying "Meditation in Progress: Please Wait Outside" for late students (or tell the students at the start of the semester that if the door is closed, come in quietly). Also, consider closing the door, shutting off any technology (overhead projectors, etc.), and dimming the lights, as this can help create a meditative atmosphere and reduce distractions.

After the students enter the classroom, begin the facilitation by saying:

Before we start the class and engage in learning, I'd like to again *invite* everyone to participate in a meditation.

(*Note:* At this point, you can reiterate the entry point used during Day 1. For example, if you described how meditation can assist with stress and anxiety, you can revisit that theme. Perhaps share a specific study or personal example.)

Again, I want to be clear that meditating in class is completely voluntary and there's no requirement to practice. You can think of this as quiet reflection time before we start learning new content. If you choose, you can listen to music quietly, engage in prayer, reflect, or sketch or draw, whatever you decide.

Regardless of your choice, we must maintain a quiet environment for the next few minutes—so please no talking, no loud music, etc.

Then, go through the following instructions for the actual meditation technique:

1. Say: "I'd like to *invite* you to put away your technology for a minute. Let's give the mind a brief rest by giving our phones and laptops a rest. I'm going to turn off or dim the lights, just so it helps create a calming atmosphere."
2. Say: "As we practiced during the last class, I'm going to ring the bowl (or chime). I'd like you to simply listen to the sound as it drops off. You can also listen to 'what remains' after the sound of the bowl disappears."
3. Say: "Remember, a comfortable posture helps. Try sitting upright but not stiff. Have your feet planted on the floor. You can let your hands rest easily in your lap. If you are comfortable, it may help to close your eyes, or you can softly cast them downward."
4. Ring the bowl or chime.
5. Wait about 30 seconds to a minute after the sound of the bowl fades away. Then, instruct the students to "gradually" come out of the meditation by slowly opening their eyes, blinking them if that helps. They can stretch the body.

Day 3

(Total time: 3–4 minutes)

Note: After being introduced to sound meditation and establishing a foundation, the students will then begin to practice breath meditation, or *vipassana* (see Chapter 4), where they focus on the natural inhalation and exhalation of the breath.

After the students enter the classroom, begin by saying:

I'd like to again *invite* everyone to participate in a short meditation. However, this time, we are going to practice what is known as mindfulness breath meditation, or *vipassana*, which originates from the Buddhist tradition but has been implemented in many facets of Western society, such as education, business, sports, counseling, and the medical field.

With this method, we listen to the sound of the bowl but then gently turn our attention to the natural flow of the in-breath and out-breath. We can think of watching or witnessing the breath in its natural state. The key is to not manipulate the breath or try to make something happen; rather, we are dropping in on what is already happening and being mindful of what is.

Finally, it's important to bring a nonjudgmental attitude and kind awareness to your practice of meditation. The ideal attitude toward meditation is one of playfulness or being easy and relaxed about it—this allows the meditation to happen spontaneously.

No matter what technique you use, there are three essential elements to remember with meditation: (1) being in a relaxed state, (2) watching or witnessing thoughts and what is happening, and (3) not evaluating or judging thoughts or the experience.

(*Note:* At this point in the facilitation, you might want to address possible unpleasant experiences during meditation and provide a *trigger warning*. See Chapter 5 for more information.)

Then, go through these steps for *vipassana*:

1. Say: "Sit with the back straight but not stiff. Have your feet planted on the floor. Allow your hands to rest easily in your lap, either cupped or with palms facing up. Allow your eyes to close or look downward. Notice, just by the way you are seated, if you can sense a feeling of centeredness and presence. If not, see if slightly adjusting your posture helps."
2. Ring the bowl or chime.
3. After the sound begins to fade, say, "Now, gently turn your attention to the breath as it flows in and out. There is a natural rhythm to the breath. Just observe or listen to this rhythm, without trying to change it. Just observe what is happening."

As the facilitator, sit quietly and observe the students. Allow them a minute or two—whatever time you can—to meditate.

4. Say: "I'm going to ring the bowl (or chime) as a way to indicate that the meditation is ending. Please take your time in coming out of the meditation." Instruct the students to "gradually" come out of the meditation by slowly opening their eyes, blinking them if that helps. They can stretch the body.
5. Ask, "Did anyone have any thoughts or become distracted during the meditation?" This is completely natural. There is a misconception that meditation involves completely clearing the mind of thoughts. Meditation is not the same as concentration; concentration involves excluding stimuli or narrowing our awareness. Meditation, in the way we are practicing it, is just the opposite—it's inclusive. Our awareness is

open to whatever occurs. We just the breath as a gentle support or frame of reference. Trying to stop or eliminate thoughts is like trying to stop your heart from beating. If we are patient, however, and simply witness our thoughts passing, in time they begin to slow down. In meditation, we bring a nonjudgmental, open attitude to thoughts—meaning, if we have thoughts or become distracted from the breath, it's no big deal. Anytime we become lost in thought or unfocused, we can very easily return to the breath.

Day 4

(Total time: 3–4 minutes)

After the students enter the classroom, begin by saying:

> I'd like to again *invite* everyone to participate in a short meditation. We are going to continue practicing mindfulness breath meditation.
>
> Again, we listen to the sound of the bowl but then gently turn our attention to the natural flow of the in-breath and out-breath. We can think of watching or observing the breath in its natural state—or you can think of it as listening to your breath. The key is to not manipulate the breath or try to make something happen; rather, we are dropping in on what is already happening and being mindful of what is.
>
> Finally, it's important to bring a nonjudgmental attitude to your practice. Again, it helps to be playful and relaxed about meditation.

Then, go through the following steps:

1. Say: "Sit with the back straight but not stiff. Have your feet planted on the floor. Allow your hands to rest easily in your lap, either cupped or with palms facing up. Allow your eyes to close or look downward. Notice, just by the way you are seated, if you can sense a feeling of centeredness and presence." Remember, in meditation, we bring a nonjudgmental, open attitude to thoughts—meaning, if we have thoughts or become distracted from the breath, it's "no big deal." Anytime we become lost in thought or unfocused, we can very easily return to the breath.
2. Ring the bowl or chime.
3. After the sound begins to fade, say, "Now, gently turn your attention to the breath as it flows in and out. There is a natural rhythm to the breath. Just observe or listen to this rhythm." As the facilitator, sit quietly and

observe the students. Allow them a minute or two—whatever time you can—to meditate.

4. Say: "I'm going to ring the bowl to indicate that the meditation is ending. Please take your time in coming out of the meditation." Instruct the students to gradually come out of the meditation by slowly opening their eyes, blinking them if that helps. They can stretch the body.

Day 5

(Total time: 3–4 minutes)

Note: The students are now introduced to a brief body scan meditation (see Chapter 4 for more explanation).

After the students enter the classroom, begin by saying:

I'd like to again *invite* everyone to participate in a short meditation. We are going to continue practicing mindfulness breath meditation, but we are going to add what is known as a body scan. This involves placing our attention on the body, just acknowledging sensations, tension—whatever is occurring.

Then, go through these steps:

1. Say: "Sit with the back straight but not stiff. Have your feet planted on the floor. Allow your hands to rest easily in your lap, either cupped or with palms facing up. Allow your eyes to close or look downward. Notice, just by the way you are seated, if you can sense a feeling of centeredness and presence."
2. Ring the bowl or chime.
3. After the sound begins to fade, say: "Now, gently turn your attention to the breath as it flows in and out. There is a natural rhythm to the breath. Just observe or listen to this rhythm."
4. Say: "Now, gently bring your attention to your neck and shoulders. Allow your mind to settle there. If you notice any tension or stress, see if you can gently release it. Now, place your attention on the palms of your hands, allowing your hands to relax. Next, bring your awareness to your stomach, and notice any tightness or tension. Finally, bring your attention to your legs and feet. Notice any tightness or tension."
5. Say: "I'm going to ring the bowl as a way to indicate that the meditation is ending. Please take your time in coming out of the meditation." Instruct the students to "gradually" come out of the meditation by slowly opening their eyes, blinking them if that helps. They can stretch the body.

Day 6

(Total time: 4–5 minutes)

Note: Repeat Day 5, continuing to focus on the body scan.
After the students enter the classroom, begin by saying:

I'd like to *invite* everyone to participate in a brief meditation.

Then, go through the steps:

1. Say: "Assume a comfortable position."
2. Ring the bowl or chime.
3. After the sound begins to fade, say: "Now, gently turn your attention to the breath as it flows in and out. There is a natural rhythm to the breath. Just observe or listen to this rhythm."
4. Say: "Now, gently bring your attention to your neck and shoulders. Allow your mind to settle there. If you notice any tension or stress, see if you can gently release it. Now, place your attention on the palms of your hands, allowing your hands to relax. Next, bring your awareness to your stomach, and notice any tightness or tension. Finally, bring your attention to your legs and feet. Notice any tightness or tension."
5. Ring the bowl or chime to end the meditation.

Day 7

(Total time: 4–5 minutes)

Note: Repeat Days 5 and 6, continuing to focus on the body scan.
After the students enter the classroom, begin by saying:

I'd like to *invite* everyone to participate in a brief meditation.

Then, go through the steps:

1. Say: "Assume a comfortable position."
2. Ring the bowl or chime.
3. After the sound begins to fade, say: "Now, gently turn your attention to the breath as it flows in and out. There is a natural rhythm to the breath. Just observe or listen to this rhythm."
4. Say: "Now, gently bring your attention to your neck and shoulders. Allow your mind to settle there. If you notice any tension or stress, see

if you can gently release it. Now, place your attention on the palms of your hands, allowing your hands to relax. Next, bring your awareness to your stomach, and notice any tightness or tension. Finally, bring your attention to your legs and feet. Notice any tightness or tension."

5. Ring the bowl or chime to end the meditation.

Day 8

(Total time: 4–5 minutes)

Note: Repeat Days 5, 6, and 7, continuing to focus on the body scan. After the students enter the classroom, begin by saying:

I'd like to *invite* everyone to participate in a brief meditation.

Then, go through the steps:

1. Say: "Assume a comfortable position."
2. Ring the bowl or chime.
3. After the sound begins to fade, say: "Now, gently turn your attention to the breath as it flows in and out. There is a natural rhythm to the breath. Just observe or listen to this rhythm."
4. Say: "Now, gently bring your attention to your neck and shoulders. Allow your mind to settle there. If you notice any tension or stress, see if you can gently release it. Now, place your attention on the palms of your hands, allowing your hands to relax. Next, bring your awareness to your stomach, and notice any tightness or tension. Finally, bring your attention to your legs and feet. Notice any tightness or tension."
5. Ring the bowl or chime to end the meditation.

Day 9 and Beyond

Note: Now that the students have a foundation for meditation, you can introduce some variations. The following are some examples to enhance the meditation (see Chapter 8 for descriptions of each activity or meditation method).

Variation 1:

Have the students practice a loving-kindness meditation.
   Follow these steps:

1. Say: "Assume a comfortable position."

2. Ring the bowl or chime.
3. After the sound begins to fade, say: "Now, gently turn your attention to the breath as it flows in and out. There is a natural rhythm to the breath. Just observe or listen to this rhythm."
4. Say: "Now, bring your attention to the heart area, in your chest. Just be aware of any sensations in that area."
5. Say: "Repeat the following phrases silently to yourself, as you gently breathe in and out: *May I be happy. May I be well. May I be peaceful.*"
6. Say: "Experience how you feel after repeating these phrases. Keep your awareness in the heart area." *Note:* If time permits, you can extend the meditation by saying: "Now, I'd like you to think of a person—a family member, friend, teacher—or being (such as a pet) that brings you happiness when you think of them. Imagine they are sitting in front of you. Silently repeat the phrase *May you be happy, may you be well* to them."
7. Ring the bowl or chime to end the meditation.

Variation 2

Invite the students outside the classroom to engage in walking meditation (for a full description of this practice, see Chapter 7).

1. Say: "Today, we are going to try something different. We are going to practice meditation while moving. When I ring the bell (or chime), I want you to walk alone, without talking or using your cell phone, in any direction that you want. Intentionally walk slowly, paying attention to how your foot meets the ground with each step. Allow your awareness to pick up any sights, sounds, or smells. When I ring the bowl (or chime), please walk back toward me."
2. Allow the students to walk for a few minutes.
3. Ring the bowl or chime to indicate that it's time to walk back toward you.

Variation 3

Have the students engage in Zen Doodling in this class.

1. Say: "Today, we will be sketching or doodling as a way to practice a meditative mindset and prepare our minds for class." (See "Zen Doodling" in Chapter 7.)
2. Provide each student with a blank piece of paper. Make sure they have a writing utensil.
3. Have them draw three large circles on their paper.
4. Say: "When I ring the bowl (or chime), begin making patterns within one of the circles, then move to fill the other two circles. You can make

whatever designs come to mind. Also, as you doodle, listen to the sound of the pen or pencil as it moves across the paper. Feel it in your hand. Watch closely as shapes and patterns take form."

5. Allow the students a few minutes to doodle, then ring the bowl or chime to indicate that the activity is finished.

Chapter 10

Spreading Meditation
across Campus

With the meditation facilitation guide in hand, you are ready to embed meditation into your classroom. You have another pedagogical tool, one that can help students adjust to instruction, de-stress, and recharge their minds. But what if you want to spread the meditative "wealth"? What if you see results and, out of your enthusiasm and concern, want to share these insights with faculty and staff across your campus? How do you make meditation part of the culture and weave it into the fabric of the college or university? This chapter will address those questions by covering strategies such as meditation faculty circles, meditation meet-ups, and establishing a meditation space on campus. There are also smaller steps you can take, simple ways to infuse the practice of meditation into existing academic structures.

MEDITATION FACULTY CIRCLES

One way to spread meditation on campus is to get other faculty involved. A strategy would be to form a faculty circle or professional learning community around meditation in the classroom. Reach out and see what other faculty might be interested. Perhaps some practice meditation personally but have not tried to implement it in the classroom with students. Others might have no experience but are interested in learning. Establish a regular monthly meeting time to come together and share experiences and exchange notes. Also, share resources on meditation (including this book). Discuss what is working and what challenges the group might be having. You might even survey students and collect some data. Working with other like-minded faculty gives support, which is sometimes needed when experimenting with new or different teaching methods.

One strategy could be to create a shared Google Doc in which faculty in the circle note their weekly experiences with facilitating meditation with their students. They can jot down what seems to be working, what challenges and concerns they have, and topics they would like to discuss in more depth. When meeting, the faculty circle can then use the document as a talking point.

MEDITATION MEET-UPS

A second strategy for weaving meditation into the college culture is to organize meditation meet-ups, or informal gatherings for faculty and staff who want to socialize and meditate with others. While meditation is a solitary pursuit, there's a kind of synergy that happens when meditating with others. As Boyce (2017) states, "You can also find resolve when you meditate with other people. You get a little boost, when your energy flags, from seeing others out of the corner of your eye. The simple thought *we're in this together* makes it a human, communal thing, rather than an abstract internal pursuit" (n.p.).

Locate a place (such as a meditation space, to be discussed later in this chapter) conducive to meditation on campus. Schedule a time and date when faculty and staff can attend. Saturday mornings have worked for me. If someone in the group has experience with meditation, they can lead others through a method; or if group members have their practices, they can simply meditate together. Another idea is to invite a local meditation teacher to come to the meet-up to offer guidance.

Being academics, those in attendance might like to peruse an article or short reading on meditation, including recent neuroscience findings. You can send the article in advance and after the meditation, ask each participant to comment or ask a question about the reading. Afterward, you might serve coffee and/or tea and enjoy some snacks and social time together.

The following are some articles to get you started: "How Meditation Works," *The Atlantic,* https://www.theatlantic.com/health/archive/2013 /06/how-meditation-works/277275/; "Meditation Is Even More Powerful Than We Originally Thought," *Huffington Post*, https://www.huffpost.com /entry/meditation-reduces-stress-harvard-study_n_6109404; "Meditation Is a Political Act," *Lion's Roar*, https://www.lionsroar.com/meditation-is-a -political-act/.

MEDITATION WORKSHOPS

Hosting workshops can be an effective way to promote meditation on campus. If you have experience, you can lead workshops for students, faculty, and staff—for example, a session on the basics of meditation. One idea is to offer convocation credits for students interested in learning to meditate. For faculty, you might facilitate professional development training, sharing meditation methods and ideas on how to embed them into the classroom.

Again, if you lack experience, invite local meditation teachers or those with more experience. Through workshops, convocations, and informal meet-ups, more individuals at the college or university will learn meditation and hopefully experience the benefits. Then, when it's introduced in the classroom, students may already have some experience and some context, making the process smoother.

STUDENT MEDITATION CLUBS

Another way to spread the meditation culture is to encourage or sponsor students to start a meditation club on campus. If students have experience, they can lead weekly or monthly meditation sessions, bringing together those interested in meditation. At Bowdoin College in Maine, several students started a Mindfulness Over Matter club to connect with those wanting to regularly meet up and meditate. "It makes these mind/body practices accessible, and students love to learn from one another," said Bernie Hershberger, the college's director of counseling. "The whole campus grows more conscious bit by bit of the importance of how to pause and ease the suffering that comes from constant anxiety."

SCHEDULED VIRTUAL MEDITATION DAYS

Colleges and universities can designate certain times and days as "meditation moments," in which faculty and students stop what they are doing to engage in a short, campus-wide meditation. A "virtual" meditation using online resources such as Google Meet, Zoom, or Microsoft Teams, can be hosted—like at Georgia State University, which schedules Meditation Monday at noon each week so those on campus remember to "take a moment" for themselves.

A MEDITATION SPACE

Another strategy for encouraging meditation on campus is to create a meditation space. This involves establishing a physical space conducive to meditation and contemplative activities that students, faculty, and staff can utilize individually or congregate in for meditation workshops or meet-ups. Dozens of higher education institutions have created meditation spaces, including Mount Holyoke College, Carnegie Mellon University, and the University of Redlands (for a complete list, see http://www.bestcounselingschools.org /best-campus-meditation-spaces/). In addition to providing a physical location, a meditation space makes a symbolic statement: *Meditation, reflection, and other contemplative practices are valued here.* At Wesleyan College, a private institution in Macon, Georgia, with the help of staff and faculty, I designed a meditation space using a vacant office on the top floor of the college's Student Services building (see following images). The room is used for individuals wanting to meditate or just have a quiet space during regular business hours, and for meditation classes, workshops, and meet-ups for faculty.

The following is a brief guide for designing a meditation space on a modest budget (about $1,200).

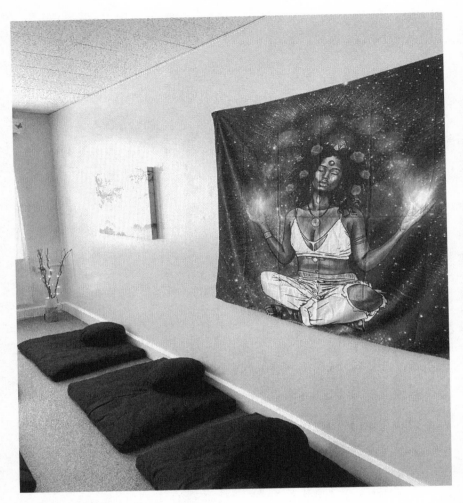

Wesleyan College's Meditation Space

Steps to Creating a Meditation Space

1. Work with college administration to determine a location for the space. Consider available space on campus but also how many individuals should fit comfortably in the space. Outdoor meditation spaces are also an option; however, weather and time of day can impact their use.
2. Creatively design the space on paper. Sketch out what it will look like. Consult the college's marketing experts and others who might help with the design and aesthetics of the space. At Wesleyan College, for

instance, the aim was to create a space that was meditative and calming but also a bit modern and relatable for students.

3. Based on your design, estimate the costs for the project. Consider items such as meditation mats, chairs, paint, wall decor, and curtains. To give you an idea of the costs, this was the budget for Wesleyan's meditation space:
   - Zen meditation mats (zafu and zabuton): $60 each x 12 = $720
   - Paint supplies (for walls): $300
   - Wall art: $60
   - Other decor (curtains, statues, water fountain, lighting): $150
   - Total cost: $1,230

4. Purchase the materials. Recruit help! Invite faculty and students to assist with painting, for instance.

5. Complete the project. Hold an open house or a meditation meet-up to promote the space.

OTHER THINGS YOU CAN DO TO PROMOTE MEDITATION

You can also encourage meditation in smaller ways that take little time and no money. You can *insert* meditation into many of the existing programs and structures at your college or university. Here are some ideas.

Faculty Meetings

If faculty meetings (or other meetings) at your college begin with an innovation or silent reflection, volunteer to facilitate a mini-meditation. Bring a singing bowl or chime and instruct faculty to mindfully listen to the sound while sitting comfortably.

Faculty Professional Development

If comfortable, offer to host a session during faculty development days that dives into meditation for self-care and well-being or is targeted toward starting classes with meditation.

First-Year Student Courses

Many higher education institutions require students to complete first-year experience courses, which provide study skills, time management, and self-care strategies. Work with the appropriate administration and faculty to build in meditation as part of the first-year curriculum.

REVISITING THE CONCEPT OF "INVITING"

As mentioned earlier in this book, it's important to approach all of these strategies with the spirit of inviting faculty, staff, and students to experience meditation. Keep it light and playful, and speak of the benefits. Don't push too hard. We have to remember that not everyone will want to meditate for various reasons—and we must respect that. Gently sharing a meditation culture will likely be the most effective way to spread the wealth.

MEDITATION IN THE COLLEGE
CLASSROOM: FINAL THOUGHTS

Those of us working in higher education are in interesting times. Students are coming to us more stressed, more anxious, and more distracted than ever. Intuitively, you might feel that *something else is needed.* As faculty, we need to add to our teaching toolkits, and what's needed is not how to deliver more content necessarily but how to better prepare the mind to receive that content. What's needed is not more seeds but more fertile soil.

Meditation in the classroom simply makes sense. Taking a few moments to just be, to settle, to center is a strategic, intelligent use of time, one that helps honor students as human beings. This small activity says: *We value you enough to give you a breather, to take a moment to collect yourself.* Taking this moment also nurtures you, as the instructor. It allows you to center, to help be your best for the people sitting in front of you.

You now have the knowledge and means to make this happen. You've gained a clear understanding of what meditation is and what it is not. You've hopefully embarked on your own practice and begun to familiarize yourself with a specific meditation method or two that you can share with students. You have contemplated how to create an ideal environment for meditation in the college classroom and determined how to strategically connect the benefits of meditation to your students' interests and life goals.

You have reflected on to what degree you want to implement meditation— maybe next semester you will feel comfortable to just ring a bell and ask students to listen. And you will take it from there. Maybe you have recruited several faculty to join you in this adventure, and you plan to meet up regularly to discuss your results. Who knows, perhaps you even have a goal to establish a meditation space on campus in the coming year.

Regardless of what you do, take small risks with your teaching, enjoy yourself, contribute to the greater good, and above all, don't forget every so often to stop and breathe—to just be.

CHAPTER SUMMARY

- Spread meditation across campus through faculty circles, meditation meet-ups, and workshops.
- Encourage or sponsor student meditation clubs.
- Work with administration to have a scheduled meditation day using virtual resources.
- Establish a meditation space on campus.
- Look for ways to include meditation in existing academic structures.

Resources

This section features a list of resources—organizations, teachers, books, and websites—that I have found helpful regarding meditation and incorporating meditation in the college classroom.

Organization

The Association for the Contemplative Mind in Higher Education (ACMHE). An initiative of the Center for Contemplative Mind in Society, ACMHE is a professional academic association established in the 1990s. The group's focus on contemplative practices, including meditation, span K–12, undergraduate, and graduate levels. ACMHE offers workshops, webinars, and conferences. More information about membership with the association can be found at https://acmhe.org/about/.

Books

Contemplative Practices in Higher Education: Powerful Methods to Transform Teaching and Learning by Daniel P. Barbezat and Mirabai Bush. This book superbly describes the theoretical underpinnings of contemplative practices in higher education but also presents specific examples and explanations of various methods and practices, from meditation to mindfulness to contemplative movement and arts.

Contemplative Practices, Pedagogy, and Research in Education by Elizabeth Dorman, Kathryn Byrnes, and Jane Dalton. This three-volume edited book series covers contemplative practices within education and the preparation of teachers. While niched in teacher education, the book is packed with examples of how meditation, mindfulness, and other contemplative practices can be introduced into the higher education classroom.

Meditation and the Classroom: Contemplative Pedagogy for Religious Studies by Judith Simmer-Brown and Fran Grace. This edited text paints an overall picture of contemplative practices happening in higher education classrooms. It gives examples of faculty from a variety of backgrounds and fields using meditation and other methods with students.

The Mindful Twenty-Something: Life Skills to Handle Stress . . . and Everything Else by Holly Rogers. This book is written with undergraduate students in mind. It makes mindfulness and meditation relatable to college students.

Stay Woke: A Meditation Guide for the Rest of Us by Justin Michael Williams. This book provides a fresh look at meditation, written in a style for those in younger generations who might be resistant to trying or establishing a practice.

The Warrior's Meditation: The Best-Kept Secret in Self-Improvement, Cognitive Enhancement, and Stress Relief by Richard Haight. In this book, Haight, an expert on Japanese samurai arts and a meditation teacher, presents a refreshing view of meditation as not fixed to forms and traditions but rather a state of awareness that can be reached more naturally through the five senses.

TEACHERS

Miles Neale is a Buddhist psychotherapist, author, and recognized speaker, who has shared many free resources that can be found on his website, https://www.milesneale.com/. There are also a number of excellent guided meditation videos posted to YouTube. Here are some:

Brief Loving-Kindness Meditation: https://www.youtube.com/watch?v=2qP2i7cKln4

Brief Mindfulness of Breathing Meditation: https://www.youtube.com/watch?v=72lKvdjYri0&t=155s

Four Applications of Mindfulness: https://www.youtube.com/watch?v=E7W9XK-b5nQ&t=613s

Mindfulness-Based Meditation: https://www.youtube.com/watch?v=F_raEsxvjh8

Sharon Salzberg, Jack Kornfield, and Joseph Goldstein founded the Insight Meditation Society in 1975. These three meditation teachers provide a wealth of resources and knowledge on meditation and mindfulness. Below are some guided meditations that are available on YouTube:

10-Minute Lovingkindness Meditation with Sharon Salzberg

Calm and Ease Meditation—Jack Kornfield

Guided Mindfulness of Breathing Meditation with Joseph Goldstein (Satipatthana Sutta)

Justin Michael Williams is an artist, author, and speaker who teaches meditation. He provides a fresh, modern approach to meditation that connects with younger generations, including college students. His website is www.justinmichaelwilliams.com/ and here are a few of his meditation-related videos on YouTube:

https://www.youtube.com/watch?v=64z2V83cm98
https://www.youtube.com/watch?v=6aVc-3G53q4
https://www.youtube.com/watch?v=4jEZtK-THDk

References

Abbott, K. A., Shanahan, M. J., & Neufeld, R. W. (2013). Artistic tasks outperform nonartistic tasks for stress reduction. *Art Therapy, 30*(2), 71–78.

Alhawatmeh, H. N., Rababa, M., Alfaqih, M., Albataineh, R., Hweidi, I., & Awwad, A. A. (2022). The benefits of mindfulness meditation on trait mindfulness, perceived stress, cortisol, and c-reactive protein in nursing students: A randomized controlled trial. *Advances in Medical Education and Practice, 13*, 47.

American College Health Association. (2010). American College Association—National College Health Assessment 2010 National Data. Hanover, Maryland.

American College Health Association. (2016). National College Health Assessment: Spring 2016 reference group executive summary. Retrieved from http://www.achancha.org/docs/NCHAII%20SPRING%20 2016%20US%20REFERENCE%20 GROUP%20 EXECUTIVE%20SUMMARY.Pdf

American Psychological Association. (2019). Mindfulness meditation: A research-proven way to reduce stress. Retrieved from: https://www.apa.org/topics /mindfulness/meditation

American Psychological Association. (2020). Stress in American 2020: A mental health crisis. Retrieved from https://www.apa.org/news/press/releases/stress/2020/ sia-mental-health-a crisis.pdf

Arias, A. J., Steinberg, K., Banga, A., & Trestman, R. L. (2006). Systematic review of the efficacy of meditation techniques as treatments for medical illness. *Journal of Alternative & Complementary Medicine, 12*(8), 817–832.

Arnett J. J. (2000). Emerging adulthood: A theory of development from the late teens through the twenties. *The American psychologist, 55*(5), 469–480.

Austin, J. H. (1998). *Zen and the brain: Toward an understanding of meditation and consciousness*. MIT Press.

Bagga, O. P., & Gandhi, A. (1983). A comparative study of the effect of Transcendental Meditation and Shavasana practice on the cardiovascular system. *Indian Heart Journal, 35*, 39–45.

Bamber, M. D., & Schneider, J. K. (2016). Mindfulness-based meditation to decrease stress and anxiety in college students: A narrative synthesis of the research. *Educational Research Review, 18*, 1–32.

Bamber, M. D., & Schneider, J. K. (2020). College students' perceptions of mindfulness-based interventions: A narrative review of the qualitative research. *Current Psychology*, 1–14.

Banerjee, M, Cavanagh, K., & Strauss, C. (2017). A qualitative study with health-care staff exploring the facilitators and barriers to engaging in a self-help mindfulness-based intervention. *Mindfulness*, 8(6), 1653–1664.

Baranski, M. F., & Was, C. A. (2019). Can mindfulness meditation improve short-term and long- term academic achievement in a higher-education course? *College Teaching*, 67(3), 188–195.

Barbezat, D. P., & Bush, M. (2013). *Contemplative practices in higher education: Powerful methods to transform teaching and learning.* John Wiley & Sons.

Belshee, A. (2005, July). Promiscuous pairing and beginner's mind: Embrace inexperience [agile programming]. In *Agile Conference, 2005. Proceedings* (pp. 125–131). IEEE.

Bergen-Cico, D., Possemato, K., & Pigeon, W. (2014). Reductions in cortisol associated with primary care brief mindfulness program for veterans with PTSD. *Medical Care, 52*, S25–S31. https://doi.org/10.1097/mlr.0000000000000224

Bilton, N. (2019). Part of the daily American diet, 34 gigabytes of data. Retrieved from: https://www.nytimes.com/2009/12/10/technology/10data.html

Birnbaum, L. (2008). The use of mindfulness training to create an "accompanying place" for social work students. *Social Work Education*, 27(8), 837–852.

Blaisdell, P. (2020). College students and stress statistics during COVID-19. Retrieved from https://timely.md/blog/college-students-stress-statistics/

Blumberg, P., & Flaherty, J. A. (1985). The influence of noncognitive variables in student performance. *Journal of Medical Education, 60,* 721–723.

Bodhipaksa (2007). *Signs of progress in meditation.* Retrieved from: https://www.wildmind.org/mindfulness/three/progress

Bono, J. (2017). Psychological assessment of Transcendental Meditation. *Meditation,* 209–217.

Bostock, S., Crosswell, A. D., Prather, A. A., & Steptoe, A. (2019). Mindfulness on-the-go: Effects of a mindfulness meditation app on work stress and well-being. *Journal of Occupational Health Psychology*, 24(1), 127.

Boyce, B. (2017). The benefit of meditating alone together. Retrieved from: https://www.mindful.org/benefit-meditating-alone-together/

Brefczynski-Lewis, J. A., Lutz, A., Schaefer, H. S., Levinson, D. B., & Davidson, R. J. (2007). Neural correlates of attentional expertise in long-term meditation practitioners. *Proceedings of the National Academy of Sciences*, 104(27), 11483–11488.

Brendel, W., & Cornett-Murtada, V. (2019). Professors practicing mindfulness: An action research study on transformed teaching, research, and service. *Journal of Transformative Education*, 17(1), 4–23.

Brown, D., Forte, M., & Dysart, M. (1984a). Differences in visual sensitivity among mindfulness meditators and non-meditators. *Perceptual and Motor Skills, 58,* 727–733.

Brown, D., Forte, M., & Dysart, M. (1984b). Visual sensitivity and mindfulness meditation. *Perceptual and Motor Skills, 58,* 775–784.

Brownell, S. E., & Tanner, K. D. (2012). Barriers to faculty pedagogical change: Lack of training, time, incentives, and . . . tensions with professional identity? *CBE—Life Sciences Education, 11*(4), 339–346.

Bush, M. (2013). Mindfulness in higher education. In *Mindfulness* (pp. 183–197). Routledge.

Cahn, B. R., & Polich, J. (2006). Meditation states and traits: EEG, ERP, and neuro-imaging studies. *Psychological Bulletin, 132*(2), 180.

Caldwell, K., Harrison, M., Adams, M., & Triplett, N. T. (2009). Effect of Pilates and Taiji Quan training on self-efficacy, sleep quality, mood, and physical performance of college students. *Journal of Bodywork and Movement Therapies, 13*(2), 155–163.

Cardoso, R., de Souza, E., Camano, L., & Leite, J. R. (2004). Meditation in health: An operational definition. *Brain Research Protocols, 14*(1), 58–60.

Carlson, L. E., Doll, R., Stephen, J., Faris, P., Tamagawa, R., Drysdale, E., & Speca, M. (2013). Randomized controlled trial of mindfulness-based cancer recovery versus supportive expressive group therapy for distressed survivors of breast cancer. *Journal of Clinical Oncology, 31*, 3119–3126. https://doi.org/10.1200/JCO.2012.47.5210

Chambers, R., Lo, B. C. Y., & Allen, N. B. (2008). The impact of intensive mindfulness training on attentional control, cognitive style, and affect. *Cognitive Therapy and Research, 32*(3), 303–322.

Chan, D., & Woollacott, M. (2007). Effects of level of meditation experience on attentional focus: Is the efficiency of executive or orientation networks improved? *The Journal of Alternative and Complementary Medicine, 13*(6), 651–658.

Clabaugh, A., Duque, J. F., & Fields, L. J. (2021). Academic stress and emotional well-being in United States college students following onset of the COVID-19 pandemic. *Frontiers in Psychology, 12.*

Clark, E. J., & Rieker, P. P. (1986). Gender differences in relationships and stress of medical and law students. *Journal of Medical Education, 61,* 32–40.

Clave-Brule, M., Mazloum, A., Park, R. J., Harbottle, E. J., & Birmingham, C. L. (2009). Managing anxiety in eating disorders with knitting. *Eating and Weight Disorders—Studies on Anorexia, Bulimia and Obesity, 14*(1), e1–e5.

Cohen-Katz, J., Wiley, S., Capuano, T., Baker, D. M., Deitrick, L., & Shapiro, S. (2005). The effects of mindfulness-based stress reduction on nurse stress and burn-out: A qualitative and quantitative study, part II I. *Holistic Nursing Practice, 19*(2), 78–86.

Colzato, L. S., & Kibele, A. (2017). How different types of meditation can enhance athletic performance depending on the specific sport skills. *Journal of Cognitive Enhancement, 1*(2), 122–126.

Course Hero. (2020). Faculty wellness and careers. Retrieved from: https://www.coursehero.com/blog/faculty-wellness-research/

Cranson. R. W., Orme-Johnson, D. W., Gackenbach, J., et al. (1991). Transcendental meditation and improved performance on intelligence-related measures: A longitudinal study. *Personality and Individual Differences, 12*, 1105–1116.

Creswell, J. D., Way, B. M., Eisenberger, N. I., & Lieberman, M. D. (2007). Neural correlates of dispositional mindfulness during affect labeling. *Psychosomatic Medicine*, *69*(6), 560–565.

Dalbec, M. (n.d.). *Meditation and journaling: Combining practices to reflect your inner world*. Retrieved from: https://kripalu.org/resources/meditation-and -journaling-combining-practices-reflect-your-inner-world

Daudén Roquet, C., & Sas, C. (2018, April). Evaluating mindfulness meditation apps. In *Extended Abstracts of the 2018 CHI Conference on Human Factors in Computing Systems* (pp. 1–6).

Davidson, R. (2003). Alterations in brain and immune function produced by mindfulness meditation. *Psychosomatic Medicine, 66*(1), 148–149.

Davidson, R. J., Kabat-Zinn, J., Schumacher, J., Rosenkranz, M., Muller, D., Santorelli, S. F., & Sheridan, J. F. (2003). Alterations in brain and immune function produced by mindfulness meditation. *Psychosomatic Medicine*, *65*(4), 564–570.

Davidson, S. (2017). Trauma-informed practices for postsecondary education: A guide. *Education Northwest*, 1–28.

Delello, Julie A., Reichard, Carla A., & Mokhtari, Kouider. (2016). Multitasking among college students: Are freshmen more distracted? *International Journal of Cyber Behavior, Psychology and Learning 6*(4), 1–12.

Ding, X., Tang, Y. Y., Tang, R., & Posner, M. I. (2014). Improving creativity performance by short-term meditation. *Behavioral and Brain Functions*, *10*(1), 1–8.

Domash, L. H. (1975). The Transcendental Meditation technique and quantum physics: Is pure consciousness a macroscopic quantum state in the brain? *Scientific Research on the Transcendental Meditation Program: Collected Papers*, *1*, 652–670.

Dove, P. (2017). How laughter leads you to deep meditation. Retrieved from: https: //www.huffpost.com/entry/how-laughter-leads-you-to-deep-meditation_b_59a0c8 1ee4b0a62d0987af2c

Dusselier, L., Dunn, B., Yongyi W., Shelley, M., II, & Whalen, D. (2005). Personal, health, academic, and environmental predictors of stress in residence halls. *Journal of American College Health, 54*(1), 15–24.

Eberth, J., & Sedlmeier, P. (2012). The effects of mindfulness meditation: A meta-analysis. *Mindfulness*, *3*(3), 174–189.

Ellerton, K. (2021). The seven vital attributes that every meditation teacher must have (and how to develop them). Retrieved from: https://kevinellerton.com/seven -attributes-meditation-teacher/

Ferreira-Vorkapic, C., Borba-Pinheiro, C. J., Marchioro, M., & Santana, D. (2018). The impact of yoga Nidra and seated meditation on the mental health of college professors. *International journal of yoga*, *11*(3), 215.

Fessenden, M. (2015). What does neuroscience know about meditation? Retrieved from: /www.smithsonianmag.com/smart-news/what-neuroscience-does -know-about-meditation-180956435/

Friedman-Wheeler, D. G., Reese, Z. A., McCabe, J. A., Yarrish, C. M., Chapagain, S., Scherer, A. M., et al. (2021). Mindfulness meditation intervention in the college classroom: Mindful awareness, working memory, content retention, and elaboration. *Scholarship of Teaching and Learning in Psychology*. Advance online publication. https://doi.org/10.1037/stl0000305

Gál, É., Ştefan, S., & Cristea, I. A. (2021). The efficacy of mindfulness meditation apps in enhancing users' well-being and mental health related outcomes: A meta-analysis of randomized controlled trials. *Journal of Affective Disorders, 279*, 131–142.

Galatzer-Levy, I. R., Burton, C. L., & Bonanno, G. A. (2012). Coping flexibility, potentially traumatic life events, and resilience: A prospective study of college student adjustment. *Journal of Social and Clinical Psychology, 31*(6), 542–567.

Glickman, M. (2002). *Beyond the breath: Extraordinary mindfulness through whole-body Vipassana meditation*. Tuttle Publishing.

Goldsby, T. L., Goldsby, M. E., McWalters, M., & Mills, P. J. (2017). Effects of singing bowl sound meditation on mood, tension, and well-being: An observational study. *Journal of Evidence-Based Complementary & Alternative Medicine, 22*(3), 401–406.

Grace, F. (2011). Learning as a path, not a goal: Contemplative pedagogy—its principles and practices. *Teaching Theology & Religion, 14*(2), 99–124.

Graves, K. (2022). Three ways to build a sustainable meditation practice. Retrieved from https://www.mindful.org/3-ways-build-sustainable-meditation-practice/#:~:text=As%20Dan%20Harris%20shares%2C%20%E2%80%9CI,mindful%2C %20is%20a%20foundational%20step.

Gray, P. (2015). Declining student resilience: A serious problem for colleges. *Psychology Today, 22*, 9–15.

Gyatso, K. (2009). *The new meditation handbook: Meditations to make our life happy and meaningful*. Tharpa Publications.

Haberlin, S. (2021). A serene segue: Examining college students' perceptions of starting classes with micro-meditations. *College Teaching*, 1–9.

Haberlin, S., Doherty, M., Donmoyer, D., Minarcine, P. M., Schwaller, T., Selke, S., Simpson Miller, B., Wilcox, V. (2022). *Brief meditation in the college classroom*. Unpublished manuscript. Faculty, Wesleyan College.

Haberlin, S., & O'Grady, P. (2018). Gifted from the "inside out": Teaching mindfulness to high-ability children. *Gifted Education International, 34*(2), 173–180.

Haight, R. (2020). *The warrior's meditation: The best-kept secret in self-improvement, cognitive enhancement, and stress relief, taught by a master of four samurai arts (total embodiment method, TEM)*. Shinkaikan Body, Mind, Spirit LLC.

Hall, P. D. (1999). The effect of meditation on the academic performance of African American college students. *Journal of black Studies, 29*(3), 408–415.

Hanh, T. N. (1998). *The heart of the Buddhas teaching*. Berkeley, CA: Parallax.

Hart, T. (2009). *From information to transformation: Education for the evolution of consciousness*. New York: Peter Lang.

Hassan, L. F. A., Rochin Demong, N. A., Mohd Salleh, M. Z., Omar, E. N., & Alwi, A. (2021). Digital addiction and the academic performance among universities' students. *Advances in Business Research International Journal, 7*(1), 189–195.

Hassed, C., & Chambers, R. (2014). *Mindful learning: Reduce stress and improve brain performance for effective learning* (Vol. 3). Exisle Publishing.

Healthline. (2016). Himalayan salt lamps: Benefits and myths. Retrieved from https://www.healthline.com/nutrition/himalayan-salt-lamp-benefits

Heckenberg, R. A., Eddy, P., Kent, S., & Wright, B. J. (2018). Do workplace-based mindfulness meditation programs improve physiological indices of stress? A systematic review and meta-analysis. *Journal of Psychosomatic Research, 114*, 62–71.

Heil, J. D. (1983). Visual imagery change during relaxation meditation training. *Dissertation Abstracts International, 43*, 2338.

Helber, C., Zook, N. A., & Immergut, M. (2012). Meditation in higher education: Does it enhance cognition? *Innovative Higher Education, 37*(5), 349–358.

Henderson, C., Finkelstein, N., & Beach, A. (2010). Beyond dissemination in college science teaching: An introduction to four core change strategies. *Journal of College Science Teaching, 39*(5), 18–25.

Herrmann, C. (1997). International experiences with the hospital anxiety and depression scale: A review of validation data and clinical results. *Journal of Psychosomatic Research, 42*(1), 17–41.

Hjeltnes, A., Binder, P. E., Moltu, C., & Dundas, I. (2015). Facing the fear of failure: An explorative qualitative study of client experiences in a mindfulness-based stress reduction program for university students with academic evaluation anxiety. *International Journal of Qualitative Studies on Health and Well-Being, 10*(1), 27990. https://doi.org/10.3402/qhw.v10.27990

Hoch, A., Stewart, D., Webb, K., & Wyandt-Hiebert, M. A. (2015, May). Trauma-informed care on a college campus. Presentation at the annual meeting of the American College Health Association, Orlando, Florida.

Hoge, E. A., Bui, E., Marques, L., Metcalf, C. A., Morris, L. K., Robinaugh, D. J., et al. (2013). Randomized controlled trial of mindfulness meditation for generalized anxiety disorder: Effects on anxiety and stress reactivity. *The Journal of Clinical Psychiatry, 74*(8), 16662.

Hölzel, B. K., Carmody, J., Vangel, M., Congleton, C., Yerramsetti, S. M., Gard, T., & Lazar, S. W. (2011). Mindfulness practice leads to increases in regional brain gray matter density. *Psychiatry Research, 191*(1), 36–43. https://doi.org/10.1016/j.pscychresns.2010.08.006

Hölzel, B. K., Lazar, S. W., Gard, T., Schuman-Olivier, Z., Vago, D. R., & Ott, U. (2011). How does mindfulness meditation work? Proposing mechanisms of action from a conceptual and neural perspective. *Perspectives on Psychological Science, 6*(6), 537–559.

Hölzel, B. K., Ott, U., Gard, T., Hempel, H., Weygandt, M., Morgen, K., & Vaitl, D. (2008). Investigation of mindfulness meditation practitioners with voxel-based morphometry. *Social Cognitive and Affective Neuroscience, 3*(1), 55–61.

Horn, A. (2020). The impact of COVID-19 on student mental health. Retrieved from https://www.activeminds.org/studentsurvey/

Horowitz, S. (2010). Health benefits of meditation: What the newest research shows. *Alternative and Complementary Therapies, 16*(4), 223–228.

Hunt, C. A., Hoffman, M. A., Mohr, J. J., & Williams, A. L. (2020). Assessing perceived barriers to meditation: The determinants of meditation practice inventory-revised (DMPI- R). *Mindfulness, 11*(5), 1139–1149.

Hussain, D., & Bhushan, B. (2010). Psychology of meditation and health: Present status and future directions. *International Journal of Psychology and Psychological Therapy*, *10*(3), 439–451.

Inácio, O., Henrique, L. L., & Antunes, J. (2006). The dynamics of Tibetan singing bowls. *Acta Acustica United with Acustica*, *92*(4), 637–653.

Jacobs, G. (2003). *The ancestral mind: A revolutionary, scientifically validated program for reactivating the deepest part of the mind.* Viking.

Jansen, E. R. (1990). *Singing bowls: A practical handbook of instruction and use.* Red Wheel/Weiser.

Jedrczak, A., Toomey, M., & Clements, G. (1986). The TM-Sidhi program, age, and brief tests of perceptual motor speed and nonverbal intelligence. *Journal of Clinical Psychology, 42*, 161–164.

Jha, A. P., Krompinger, J., & Baime, M. J. (2007). Mindfulness training modifies subsystems of attention. *Cognitive, Affective, & Behavioral Neuroscience, 7*(2), 109–119.

Johnson, J. E. (2016). Effect of mindfulness training on interpretation exam performance in graduate students in interpreting. Doctoral dissertation, University of San Francisco. Retrieved from: https:// repository.usfca.edu/cgi/viewcontent.cgi?refere r=https://scholar. google.com/&httpsredir=1&article=1310&context=diss

Josa, C. (2012). Five things you need to know about meditating on a chair. Retrieved from: http://www.clarejosa.com/about-clare-josa/

Kabat-Zinn, J. (2005). *Coming to our senses: Healing ourselves and the world through mindfulness.* Hachette UK.

Kaul, P., Passafiume, J., Sargent, R. C., & O'Hara, B. F. (2010). Meditation acutely improves psychomotor vigilance and may decrease sleep need. *Behavioral and Brain Functions*, *6*(1), 1–9.

Keithler, M. A. (1981). The influence of the transcendental meditation program and personality variables on auditory thresholds and cardio-respiratory responding. *Dissertation Abstracts International, 42*, 1662–1663.

Kindel, H. R. (2018). *Toward expert clinicians: The effects of teaching mindfulness in physical therapy education.* Robert Morris University.

Kirby, L. A., Kornman, P. T., & Robinson, J. L. (2021). Outcomes of "brain breaks": Short consistent meditation and silent sessions in the college classroom are associated with subtle benefits. *Journal of Cognitive Enhancement*, *5*(1), 99–117.

Komiya, N., Good, G. E., & Sherrod, N. B. (2000). Emotional openness as a predictor of college students' attitudes toward seeking psychological help. *Journal of Counseling Psychology*, *47*(1), 138.

Komjathy, L. (2017). *Introducing contemplative studies.* John Wiley & Sons.

Koncz, A., Demetrovics, Z., & Takacs, Z. K. (2021). Meditation interventions efficiently reduce cortisol levels of at-risk samples: A meta-analysis. *Health psychology review*, *15*(1), 56–84.

Kopec, D., Maher, M., Brower, M., and O'Hara, M. (2014). *The role of water features within the healthcare environment.* MedEd Facilities Boston.

Kuhl, M., & Boyraz, G. (2017). Mindfulness, general trust, and social support among trauma-exposed college students. *Journal of Loss and Trauma, 22*(2), 150–162.

Kulze, L. (2013). How meditation works. Retrieved from https://www.theatlantic.com/health/archive/2013/06/how-meditation-works/277275/

Kutz, I., Borysenko, J. Z., & Benson, H. (1985). Meditation and psychotherapy: A rationale for the integration of dynamic psychotherapy, the relaxation response, and mindfulness meditation. *The American Journal of Psychiatry*.

Lagopoulos, J., Xu, J., Rasmussen, I., Vik, A., Malhi, G. S., Eliassen, C. F., et al. (2009). Increased theta and alpha EEG activity during nondirective meditation. *The Journal of Alternative and Complementary Medicine, 15*(11), 1187–1192.

Lardone, A., Liparoti, M., Sorrentino, P., Rucco, R., Jacini, F., Polverino, A., Minino, R., Pesoli, M., Baselice, F., Sorriso, A., Ferraioli, G., Sorrentino, G., & Mandolesi, L. (2018). Mindfulness meditation is related to long-lasting changes in hippocampal functional topology during resting state: A magnetoencephalography study. *Neural Plasticity*, 5340717. https://doi.org/10.1155/2018/5340717

Lauricella, S. (2013). Mindfulness meditation with undergraduates in face-to-face and digital practice: A formative analysis. *Mindfulness, 5*(6), 682–688. https://doi.org/10.1007/s12671-013-0222-x

Lazar, S. W., Kerr, C. E., Wasserman, R. H., Gray, J. R., Greve, D. N., Treadway, M. T., et al. (2005). Meditation experience is associated with increased cortical thickness. *Neuroreport, 16*(17), 1893.

Lee, B. K. (Ed.). (2019). *The soul of higher education: Contemplative pedagogy, research and institutional life for the twenty-first century*. IAP.

Lemay, V., Hoolahan, J., & Buchanan, A. (2019). Impact of a yoga and meditation intervention on students' stress and anxiety levels. *American Journal of Pharmaceutical Education, 83*(5).

Lennon, E. (2021). *Five signs that your meditation practice is working*. Retrieved from: https://shedefined.com.au/wellbeing/5-signs-that-your-meditation-practice-isworking/#:~:text=People%20often%20experience%20a%20temporary,your%20meditation%20practice%20is%20working.

Levine, L. E., Waite, B. M., & Bowman, L. L. (2013). Use of instant messaging predicts self -report but not performance measures of inattention, impulsiveness, and distractibility. *Cyberpsychology, Behavior, and Social Networking, 16*(12), 898–903.

Light, R., & Jegla, A. (2022). Experimenting with teaching to improve student learning: Part 1. Retrieved from https://www.insidehighered.com/advice/2022/05/11/encouraging-faculty-try-and-test-new-teaching-strategies-opinion

Lin, J., & Parikh, R. (2019). Connecting meditation, quantum physics, and consciousness: Implication for higher education. *Contemplative Pedagogies in K–12, University, and Community Settings: Transformation for Deep Learning and Being*, 3–25.

Linden, W. (1973). Practicing of meditation by school children and their levels of field dependence independence, test anxiety, and reading achievement. *Journal of Consulting and Clinical Psychology, 41,* 139–143.

Lindquist, S. I., & McLean, J. P. (2011). Daydreaming and its correlates in an educational environment. *Learning and Individual Differences, 21*(2), 158–167.

Linn, B. S., & Zeppa, R. (1984). Stress in junior medical students: Relationship to personality and performance. *Journal of Medical Education, 59*(1), 7–12.

Lizzie, J. (2017). Stop judging and just delight in your meditation practice as it is. Retrieved from: https://www.yogapedia.com/2/6764/meditation/dont-judge -your-meditation

Lomas, T., Cartwright, T., Edginton, T., & Ridge, D. (2015). A qualitative analysis of experiential challenges associated with meditation practice. *Mindfulness, 6*(4), 848–860.

Luu, K., & Hall, P. A. (2017). Examining the acute effects of hatha yoga and mindfulness meditation on executive function and mood. *Mindfulness, 8*(4), 873–880.

Mah, L., Szabuniewicz, C., & Fiocco, A. J. (2016). Can anxiety damage the brain? *Current Opinion in Psychiatry, 29*(1), 56–63.

Maloney, E. A., Sattizahn, J. R., & Beilock, S. L. (2014). Anxiety and cognition. *Wiley Interdisciplinary Reviews: Cognitive Science, 5*(4), 403–411.

Matko, K., & Sedlmeier, P. (2019). What is meditation? Proposing an empirically derived classification system. *Frontiers in Psychology, 10*, 2276.

McDonald, K. (2005). *How to meditate: A practical guide*. Simon and Schuster.

Meade, E. (2019). The history and origin of meditation. Retrieved from https://positivepsychology.com/history-of-meditation/

Micu, A. (2019). Around one-quarter of those who meditate experience unpleasant symptoms—we don't know why. Retrieved from: https://www.zmescience.com/ science/meditation-psychological-symptoms-2322442923/

Miller, J. P. (1994). Contemplative practice in higher education: An experiment in teacher development. *Journal of Humanistic Psychology 34*(4). http://journals .sagepub.com/doi/abs/10.1177/00221678940344005

Miller, J. P., & Nozawa, A. (2002). Meditating teachers: A qualitative study. *Journal of In-Service Education, 28*(1), 179–192.

Mokhtari, K., Delello, J., & Reichard, C. (2015). Connected yet distracted: Multitasking among college students. *Journal of College Reading and Learning, 45*(2), 164–180.

Morrison, A. B., Goolsarran, M., Rogers, S. L., & Jha, A. P. (2014). Taming a wandering attention: Short-form mindfulness training in student cohorts. *Frontiers in Human Neuroscience, 7*, 897.

Mowbray, C. T., Mandiberg, J. M., Stein, C. H., Kopels, S., Curlin, C., Megivern, D., ... & Lett, R. (2006). Campus mental health services: Recommendations for change. *American Journal of Orthopsychiatry, 76*(2), 226–237.

Mrazek, M. D., Phillips, D. T., Franklin, M. S., Broadway, J. M., & Schooler, J. W. (2013). Young and restless: Validation of the Mind-Wandering Questionnaire (MWQ) reveals disruptive impact of mind-wandering for youth. *Frontiers in Psychology, 4*, 560.

MtvU, Jed Foundation, & The Associated Press. (2009). Stress and mental health poll. Retrieved from: http://www.halfofus.com/_media/_pr/may09_exec.pdf

Neale, M. (2017). In Loizzo, J. E., Neale, M. E., & Wolf, E. J. (2017). *Advances in contemplative psychotherapy: Accelerating healing and transformation*. Routledge/ Taylor & Francis Group.

Ohara, B. (2011). In Simmer-Brown, J., and F. Grace, F. (Eds.), *Meditation and the classroom: Contemplative pedagogy for religious studies.* SUNY Press.

Oman, D., Shapiro, S. L., Thoresen, C. E., Plante, T. G., & Flinders, T. (2008). Meditation lowers stress and supports forgiveness among college students: A randomized controlled trial. *Journal of American College Health, 56*(5), 569–578.

Osho. (1969). *Falling in love with darkness: Overcoming the fear of darkness and discovering its qualities of rest, relaxation, and profound peace.* Osho Media International.

Osho. (1974). *Book of secrets: 112 meditations to discover the mystery within.* Osho Media International.

Osho. (1977). *How can meditation solve life problems or prevent wars?* Osho Media International.

Osho Sammasati. (n.d.) Choosing a meditation method. Retrieved from https://oshosammasati.org/osho-meditation/choosing-meditation-method/

Ospina, M. B., Bond, K., Karkhaneh, M., Tjosvold, L., Vandermeer, B., Liang, Y., et al. (2007). Meditation practices for health: State of the research. *Evidence Report/Technology Assessment, 155,* 1–263.

Owen-Smith, P. L. (2018). *The contemplative mind in the scholarship of teaching and learning.* Indiana University Press.

Pagnoni, G., & Cekic, M. (2007). Age effects on gray matter volume and attentional performance in Zen meditation. *Neurobiology of Aging, 28*(10), 1623–1627.

Patsali, M. E., Mousa, D. P. V., Papadopoulou, E. V., Papadopoulou, K. K., Kaparounaki, C. K., Diakogiannis, I., & Fountoulakis, K. N. (2020). University students' changes in mental health status and determinants of behavior during the COVID-19 lockdown in Greece. *Psychiatry Research, 292,* 113298.

Prochnik, G. 2011. *In pursuit of silence: Listening for meaning in a world of noise.* New York: Anchor.

Ra, C. K., Cho, J., Stone, M. D., De La Cerda, J., Goldenson, N. I., Moroney, E., et al. (2018). Association of digital media use with subsequent symptoms of attention-deficit/hyperactivity disorder among adolescents. *Jama, 320*(3), 255–263.

Rajneesh, B. S. (1976). *Meditation: The art of ecstasy.* Harper & Row.

Read, J. P., Ouimette, P., White, J., Colder, C., & Farrow, S. (2011). Rates of DSM–IV–TR trauma exposure and posttraumatic stress disorder among newly matriculated college students. *Psychological Trauma: Theory, Research, Practice, and Policy, 3*(2), 148–156.

Reyes, M. (2020). Types of Christian meditation in the bible. Retrieved from: https://seattlechristiancounseling.com/articles/types-of-christian-meditation-in-the-bible

Ricard, M. (2010). *Why meditate? Working with thoughts and emotions.* Hay House, Inc.

Ricard, M. (2015). Altruism: Google talk. Retrieved from https://www.youtube.com/watch?v=jUlWDxhSlt8

Roberts, J., Yaya, L., & Manolis, C. (2014). The invisible addiction: Cell-phone activities and addiction among male and female college students. *Journal of Behavioral Addictions, 3*(4), 254–265.

Rogers, H. B. (2013). Mindfulness meditation for increasing resilience in college students. *Psychiatric Annals, 43*(12), 545–548.

Salzberg, S. (2011). Mindfulness and loving-kindness. *Contemporary Buddhism, 12*(1), 177–182.

Sandi, C. (2013). Stress and cognition. *Wiley Interdisciplinary Reviews: Cognitive Science, 4*(3), 245–261.

Schussel, L., & Miller, L. (2013). Best self visualization method with high-risk youth. *Journal of Clinical Psychology, 69*(8), 836–845.

Schwind, J. K., McCay, E., Beanlands, H., Martin, L. S., Martin, J., & Binder, M. (2017). Mindfulness practice as a teaching-learning strategy in higher education: A qualitative exploratory pilot study. *Nurse Education Today, 50*(3), 92–96. https://doi.org/10.1016/j.nedt.2016.12.017

Scott, E. (2022). How to meditate with incense. Retrieved from: https://www.verywellmind.com/meditate-with-aromatherapy-3144780

Sears, S. R., Kraus, S., Carlough, K., & Treat, E. (2011). Perceived benefits and doubts of participants in a weekly meditation study. *Mindfulness, 2*(3), 167–174.

Shapiro, S. L., Brown, K. W., & Astin, J. (2011). Toward the integration of meditation into higher education: A review of research evidence. *Teachers College Record, 113*(3), 493–528.

Shonin, E., Gordon, W., & Griffiths, M. (2013). Meditation awareness training (MAT) for improved psychological well-being: A qualitative examination of participant experiences. *Journal of Religion and Health, 53*(3), 849–863. https://doi.org/10.1007/s10943-013-9679-0

Shonk, S. M., & Cicchetti, D. (2001). Maltreatment, competency deficits, and risk for academic and behavioral maladjustment. *Developmental Psychology, 37*(1), 3–17.

Shumsky, S. (2001). *Exploring meditation: Master the ancient art of relaxation and enlightenment.* Red Wheel/Weiser.

Silva, A. (2020). *Meditation for vipassana: Guided meditation to learn the secret art of vipassana, bring clarity, focus, help declutter your mind, and renew concentration.* Adesh Silva.

Simmer-Brown, J., & Grace, F. (Eds.). (2011). *Meditation and the classroom: Contemplative pedagogy for religious studies.* SUNY Press.

Singh, N. (2014). *The psychology of meditation.* Nova Science Publishers.

Small, G. W., Lee, J., Kaufman, A., Jalil, J., Siddarth, P., Gaddipati, H., et al. (2022). Brain health consequences of digital technology use. *Dialogues in Clinical Neuroscience.*

Smyth, J. M., Hockemeyer, J. R., Heron, K. E., Wonderlich, S. A., & Pennebaker, J. W. (2008). Prevalence, type, disclosure, and severity of adverse life events in college students. *Journal of American College Health, 57*(1), 69–76.

Stew, G. (2011). Mindfulness training for occupational therapy students. *The British Journal of Occupational Therapy, 74*(6), 269–276. https://doi.org/10.4276/030802211X13074383957869

Struthers, C. W., Perry, R. P., & Menec, V. H. (2000). An examination of the relationship among academic stress, coping, motivation, and performance in college. *Research in Higher Education, 41*(5), 581–592.

Tadwalkar, R. (n.d.). 7 signs during meditation that your practice is working. Retrieved from: https://theshantipath.com/7signsmeditationworking/

Tang, Y. Y., Ma, Y., Wang, J., Fan, Y., Feng, S., Lu, Q., et al. (2007). Short-term meditation training improves attention and self-regulation. *Proceedings of the National Academy of Sciences, 104*(43), 17152–17156.

Tarrasch, R. (2015). Mindfulness meditation training for graduate students in educational counseling and special education: A qualitative analysis. *Journal of Child and Family Studies, 24*(5), 1322–1333.

Thorp, T. (2015). How to deal with emotions that arise during meditation. Retrieved from: https://www.sonima.com/meditation/emotions-during-meditation/

Travis, F., Haaga, D. A., Hagelin, J., Tanner, M., Nidich, S., Gaylord-King, C., et al. (2009). Effects of Transcendental Meditation practice on brain functioning and stress reactivity in college students. *International Journal of Psychophysiology, 71*(2), 170–176.

Travis, F., Sarina, G., & Stixrud, W. (2011). ADHD, brain functioning, and Transcendental Meditation practice. *Mind & Brain, 2*(1).

Turkle, S. *Alone together: Why we expect more from technology and less from each other.* Hachette.

Vestergaard-Poulsen, P., van Beek, M., Skewes, J., Bjarkam, C. R., Stubberup, M., Bertelsen, J., & Roepstorff, A. (2009). Long-term meditation is associated with increased gray matter density in the brain stem. *Neuroreport, 20*(2), 170–174.

Vidic, Z., & Cherup, N. (2019). Mindfulness in classroom: Effect of a mindfulness-based relaxation class on college students' stress, resilience, self-efficacy and perfectionism. *College Student Journal, 53*(1), 130–144.

Vieten, C., Wahbeh, H., Cahn, B. R., MacLean, K., Estrada, M., Mills, P., et al. (2018). Future directions in meditation research: Recommendations for expanding the field of contemplative science. *PloS ONE, 13*(11), e0205740.

Villate, V. M. (2015). Yoga for college students: An empowering form of movement and connection. *Physical Educator, 72*(1), 44.

Vipassana Research Institute. (n.d.). What is vipassana? Retrieved from: https://www.vridhamma.org/What-is-Vipassana

Walden University. (2022). How is modern technology affecting human development? Retrieved from: https://www.waldenu.edu/online-masters-programs/ms-in-developmental-psychology/resource/how-is-modern-technology-affecting-human-development

Wallace, R. K., Silver, J., Mills, P. J., Dillbeck, M. C., & Wagoner, D. E. (1983). Systolic blood pressure and long-term practice of the Transcendental Meditation and TM-Sidhi programs: Effects of TM on systolic blood pressure. *Psychosomatic Medicine.*

Walsh, R., & Shapiro, S. L. (2006). The meeting of meditative disciplines and Western psychology: A mutually enriching dialogue. *American Psychologist, 61*(3), 227.

Wang, X., Hegde, S., Son, C., Keller, B., Smith, A., & Sasangohar, F. (2020). Investigating mental health of US college students during the COVID-19 pandemic: Cross-sectional survey study. *Journal of Medical Internet Research, 22*(9), e22817.

Watts, A. (2010). *Still the mind: An introduction to meditation.* New World Library.

Williams, A. L., Dixon, J., McCorkle, R., & Van Ness, P. H. (2011). Determinants of meditation practice inventory: Development, content validation, and initial psychometric testing. *Alternative Therapies in Health and Medicine, 17*(5), 16.

Williams, R. (2018). 5 meditation styles for beginners: Choosing the right type for you. Retrieved from: https://chopra.com/articles/5-meditation-styles-for-beginners -choosing-the-right-type-for-you

Willis, J. (2014). The neuroscience behind stress and learning. Retrieved from: https: //www.edutopia.org/blog/neuroscience-behind-stress-and-learning-judy-willis

Wójcik, M., Boreński, G., Poleszak, J., Szabat, P., Szabat, M., & Milanowska, J. (2019). Meditation and its benefits. *Journal of Education, Health and Sport, 9*(9), 466–476.

Zajonc, A. (2013). Contemplative pedagogy: A quiet revolution in higher education. *New Directions for Teaching and Learning, 134,* 83–94.

Zeidan, F., Johnson, S. K., Diamond, B. J., David, Z., & Goolkasian, P. (2010). Mindfulness meditation improves cognition: Evidence of brief mental training. *Consciousness and Cognition, 19*(2), 597–605.